BYW, WHO ARE WE?

30 DEVOTIONS FOR BAPTIST YOUNG WOMEN

by Deborah P. Brunt

Woman's Missionary Union, SBC
Birmingham, Alabama

Published by Woman's Missionary Union, Auxiliary to Southern Baptist Convention, P.O. Box 830010, Birmingham, AL 35283-0010: Marjorie J. McCullough, president; Carolyn Weatherford, executive director; Bobbie Sorrill, associate executive director, Missions Education System; Lynn Yarbrough, Publications Section director; Karen C. Simons, Products Group manager.

Cindy McClain, **editor**
Christy Choyce, **editorial assistant**
Kelly Vornauf, **artist**

Brunt, Deborah P., 1954-
  BYW, who are we? : 30 devotions for Baptist young women / by Deborah P. Brunt.
     p. cm.
  ISBN 0-936625-58-9 :
  1. Young women—Prayer-books and devotions—English. 2. Women, Baptist—Prayer-books and devotions—English. 3. Baptist Young Women. I. Title.
  BV4860.B78   1989   89-31103
242'.633—dc19   CIP

W895101 • 5M • 0489
ISBN 0-936625-58-9

WHO AM I?

I am who God says I am

It was spring, my fourth-grade year. My two younger sisters and I were sick. My mother, three months pregnant with baby number four, piled us all into the car; and we set out down a rainy highway to visit a pediatrician in a city 50 miles away.

About 25 miles into our trip, an approaching car veered out of control and hit us head-on. Mama was thrown into the steering wheel. Though badly injured, she recovered. Six months later, when my baby brother was born, he bore a mark from that accident—a large cyst over one eye.

READ Ephesians 2:1-10. Underline words and phrases that describe your nature before Christ. Circle words and phrases that describe the new nature God gives.

REFLECT My brother, Jim, suffered minor injury as a result of the accident that happened before his birth. (The cyst was removed when he was a toddler.) When Adam and Eve fell, however, the nature of every unborn person suffered great damage.

Consequently, those created to reflect the image of God enter this world with natures characterized by sin. All are enslaved by the destroyer. All crave the things that destroy. "Actually all of us were like them and lived according to our natural desires, doing whatever suited the wishes of our own bodies and minds. In our natural condition we, like everyone else, were destined to suffer God's anger" (Eph. 2:3 TEV).

But God intervened. He saw the deadly defect with

1

which you were born and the destruction for which you were headed. He groaned over you as a parent over a terminally-ill child. But He did not try to "fix" your old nature. He made a way to offer you a new nature, a nature characterized by life.

He sent His Son Jesus—God from eternity past—to be born of woman and, still fully God, to become fully man. The Son lived a sinless life. Then, while still a young man, He accepted the agony and death of the cross—for you.

Have you received the new life God offers you? If so, you received it through faith in Christ Jesus. You confessed Him as your only hope. You accepted Him as your Lord. In that moment, you were created anew. Now, you are God's "workmanship" (v. 10)—His work of art, His masterpiece. You are a Designer original.

The Greek word translated *workmanship* in verse 10 is *poiema*, from which we get the English word *poem*. If you have been "created in Christ Jesus" (v. 10 NASB), you are God's poem.

Karen was eight years old when she accepted Christ. She says, "I remember sitting with Grandmother in her living room and asking her many questions about inviting Jesus into my heart. Grandmother answered them all wisely and patiently, and then we prayed together to ask Jesus to save me."

Judy knew the "plan of salvation" early in life. But, growing up, she based her relationship with God on feelings alone, rather than faith.

"The summer after my graduation from college," she recalls, "I went back to my parents' home for a rest before starting my first job. While there, I spent a great deal of time thinking about my life. I also attended a revival held by Manley Beasley. During this revival, I began to see for the first time that although I acted like a good Christian should, my life was devoid of any real faith in God.

"One day I sat and read the Bible all day, wondering, thinking, struggling. Finally, God's truth broke through my confusion and fear. I realized that the *only* way to have a relationship with God was by trusting His Son, Jesus Christ, with my life."

Both Karen and Judy now have new natures. Their lives are poems. I know. They are my sisters.

A poem flows from a poet.
  No poem ever just happened.
  None ever created itself.
A poem has meter.
  Its every syllable contributes
  to the rhythm of the whole.
Most poems have rhyme.
  A quality poem, whether rhyming or not,
  makes melody when read aloud.
A good poem paints a picture.
  It creates sharp images
  in readers' minds.

Does your life have rhythm, rhyme, message, impact? To find out, take a moment to stand back and look at yourself from the perspective of the Master Poet. Do you see a woman who has had a personal encounter with Jesus Christ? If so, God says, "You are My poem."

REPROGRAM Memorize Ephesians 2:10.
(Suggestion: Start a *BYW, Who Are We?* notebook. In it, copy memory verses, record insights, and write personal responses.)

RESPOND Write a brief prayer poem expressing who you are in God's eyes. If you have not received Christ, will you do so now? Confess to God who you are apart from Him. Ask Jesus to be your Lord. As soon as possible, seek out a mature Christian who can rejoice with you in your new life and explain to you the next steps you need to take.

D A Y 2

WHO AM I?

I am who I think I am

If someone asked you to describe yourself, using four words or phrases, what would you say? Now ask yourself, "Are these the terms God would use to describe me?"

Don't reply too quickly. First, look closely at today's Scripture passage. Notice as you read that, though Christians live in the same world as unbelievers, they are essentially different.

READ Ephesians 4:17-24. According to these verses, what part does the mind play (a) in the life of an unbeliever? (b) in the life of a Christian?

REFLECT Once you become a Christian, you will see changes in yourself, though they may come slowly. God sees sweeping changes immediately. He views you as a new creation—totally different from all persons without Christ.

In His Word, He describes you, not as you may sometimes act, but as He re-created you to be. The Bible says, for example, that you are perceptive (1 John 2:20; 1 Cor. 2:9-16), victorious (1 John 4:4; 5:4-5), and influential (Matt. 5:13-15). (You will be looking in-depth at several other things God says about you in the devotions that follow.)

Of course, your Lord knows you haven't arrived yet. He still encourages, reproves, teaches, and commands, to keep you on track. Always, though, He builds His challenge to *become* on the bedrock assurance of who you *are*:

• "Since you are God's dear children, you must try to

4

be like him" (Eph. 5:1 TEV).
- "Since you are God's people, . . . you should give thanks to God" (Eph. 5:3-4 TEV).
- "Since you have become the Lord's people, you are in the light. So you must live like people who belong to the light" (Eph. 5:8b TEV).

And that's only a sample. God has lots of terms to describe you, all of them good.

What do *you* think? Do you agree with God's assessment? Or are you skeptical when you read biblical descriptions of the people of God? Do you think, *Oh, that's not me! Maybe, someday, perhaps, I'll be like that—but certainly not any time soon.*

God promises that He will complete what He has begun in you (Phil. 1:6). Eventually, He will conform you fully to the image of Jesus. But how quickly He does His transforming work depends in large measure on you. You can short-circuit the changes He wants to work in you today by continuing to think of yourself as you have always thought.

Consider the Israelites. They had God's promise: He was going to give them Canaan. But at the border of the promised land, they turned back. They were 40 years late claiming their inheritance because they thought of themselves, not as God's overcomers, but as "grasshoppers."

When describing a selfish person, Solomon wrote: "As he thinketh in his heart, so is he" (Prov. 23:7 KJV). That principle applies just as much to today's Christian women as it did to yesterday's stingy men. To paraphrase Solomon: As a woman thinks (reckons, values herself) within herself, so is she.

In Ephesians 4:22-24, Paul wrote the same truth in a different way. He said, in effect, "To begin looking like the new person you are, you must begin thinking like the new person you are." Paul understood that your new self will hang in the closet like a dress that's never been worn until you begin to "be constantly renewed in the spirit of your mind—having a fresh mental and spiritual attitude" (v. 23 Amplified).

How do you gain a fresh attitude about yourself? You must program it in. Where do you find the material for

5

your reprogramming project? You know the answer: in God's Word.

God's thoughts about you are recorded between the covers of His Book. Those thoughts won't leap from Book to brain while you lie asleep with the Bible on your bedside table. Nor will God's thoughts imprint themselves on your mind as you snatch an occasional Scripture reading or wait to be spoon fed God's truth on Sundays.

Reprogramming requires concentrated, purposeful effort. If you want a renewed mind, you must keep putting in God's disk and turning on your computer. You must read God's Word consistently and thoroughly, mull it over, memorize it, say it aloud. You must give God time to speak to you. With God's guidance you can override the old thought patterns with new, divine ones. Only then will you begin to become who you are.

REPROGRAM   Repeat Ephesians 2:10 aloud several times. As you do so, ponder the words you are saying.

RESPOND   Commit yourself to a daily study of God's Word this month, using *BYW, Who Are We?* Pray that, through your study, you will discover thoughts about yourself that God wants you to think. Starting now, make a conscious effort to describe yourself as God does. When tempted to belittle yourself, for example, say aloud, "I am God's workmanship."

D A Y 3

WHO AM I?

I am a woman with a new heart

I cleaned the windows of our newly-built home ten months ago. Eight months pregnant with our second child at the time, I carefully carried storm windows outside and washed them down. Then, I attacked the paned windows, inside and out. (My husband handled the ones that had to be reached by ladder.) With all the dust, plaster, and grime scrubbed away, the glass "disappeared." Sunshine poured into our rooms.

I cleaned windows again yesterday. Inside, some bore baby and toddler fingerprints. Outside, many were splotched with mud. Amazingly, several still looked clean—until I wiped them and then examined the cloth. They too had accumulated a layer of filth, I realized. They too needed another washing.

READ Psalm 51:10-19. Identify (a) the kind of heart God receives, (b) the kind of heart God creates, and (c) the results of having these two heart qualities.

REFLECT Humans are born with a heart defect. It's a deadly defect, one God cannot ignore. Early in history, "The Lord saw how great man's wickedness on the earth had become, *and that every inclination of the thoughts of his heart was only evil all the time*" (Gen. 6:5 NIV, emphasis added)—and God sent the flood.

After the flood, the Lord knew that the defect remained: "Never again will I curse the ground because of man, *even though every inclination of his heart is evil from childhood*" (Gen. 8:21, NIV, emphasis added).

7

At the giving of the law, God cried: "Oh, that their hearts would be inclined to fear me and keep all my commands always, so that it might go well with them and their children forever!" (Deut. 5:29 NIV).

Later, Jeremiah asked: "Who can understand the human heart? There is nothing else so deceitful; it is too sick to be healed" (Jer. 17:9 TEV).

Perhaps David wrote of this human heart problem most personally when he penned Psalm 51. He had committed the sins of adultery and murder. He had been confronted with his actions by the prophet Nathan.

Broken-hearted, offering no excuses, David came to the Lord. Confessing his wrongdoing, he cried out, "Create a pure heart in me, O God, and put a new and loyal spirit in me" (Psalm 51:10 TEV).

God forgave David and created in him the clean heart he requested. As a result, David regained assurance of God's presence. He knew again the joy and desire to obey that he had lost while his heart was muddied with sin (vv. 11-12). He could again witness effectively (vv. 13-15) and intercede powerfully (vv. 18-19).

You have an advantage over David. Your new self created in Christ Jesus came complete with a new heart. That new heart isn't perfect yet; rather, it's redirected. You now have joys and desires that differ dramatically from those you had before accepting Christ. At the onset of your Christian experience, your new heart was clean. You had received God's forgiveness. He had washed away all sin from your life.

Yet, as a Christian, you can still sin. And when you do, your new joys and desires may get buried in mire—unless you take steps to keep your heart washed.

What steps?

1. Recognize any sin you have committed.
2. Confess it to God.
3. Receive His forgiveness and cleansing.

You probably know those steps. But are you taking them regularly? If you fail to bathe for several days, your body will begin to give off an unpleasant odor. If you duck confession of sin day after day, you will soon begin to smell spiritually. The Lord and other Christians may seem to be keeping their distance.

When you have gone without a bath for a while, you feel grimy. You may not sleep well. When you try to get by without up-to-date confession, you will carry guilt. Even if you are able to stifle that guilt most of the time, it will often surface when you lie still at night.

Having a cleansed heart ought not to be the focal point of your life, but it does need to be the starting point. You don't generally get up in the morning thinking, "Today, my goal is—a bath." Rather, you bathe in order to be ready to meet the other demands of the day.

To be ready spiritually to meet what each day holds, confess sin as soon as you are aware of it. Name the wrong you have done. By God's grace, turn from it. During your personal devotional times, ask God to pinpoint any unconfessed sin in your life. Take time to listen for His reply. If a sin or sins come to mind, deal with them.

Once you have come to God broken-hearted and received at His hands a good heart-scrubbing, you can meet life rejoicing. You can witness with new power and intercede with new passion.

You are a woman with a new heart. Don't neglect to keep it clean.

REPROGRAM   Repeat Ephesians 2:10.

RESPOND   Has God pricked you about unconfessed sin in your life? Lay it before Him now. Make Psalm 51 your personal prayer of confession to the Lord.

D A Y   4

WHO AM I?

I'm a woman with a hungry heart:
I want to know God

Your new heart in Christ has some characteristics flesh-and-blood hearts don't have. For one thing, your new heart can get hungry. Spiritually, you can yearn to know Christ much as a starving person craves food and water. Paul did. So did Mary, sister of Martha and Lazarus.

READ   Philippians 3:7-14 and Luke 10:38-42. In Philippians, circle phrases that identify Paul's desire. Underline phrases that show the intensity of that desire. In Luke, note how Mary satisfied her desire to know Jesus and what Jesus said about her actions.

REFLECT   Recall a time when you felt really hungry. How long had you gone without eating? Imagine that you have been deprived of food for 10 or 12 days. Which of the following do you think you would count most valuable: a new car, a fur coat, a diamond ring, a good meal? In other circumstances, you might value the car, coat, or ring most highly. But if you were truly starving, food alone would matter.

Paul had the same yearning to know Christ that a starving person has for food. He had previously thought other things important—his Jewish heritage and his religious zeal, for example. But when he looked at those things next to the priceless privilege of intimacy with Jesus, they looked shoddy. They lost their value in his eyes.

10

Paul already knew Christ, of course, when he penned his letter to the Philippians. The apostle had long since committed his life to the Lord Jesus. Paul knew Jesus—and that just whetted his appetite. He wanted to know Him more.

Our baby daughter, Amanda, recently had a stomach virus. She wanted to eat again before her stomach was ready to accept food. I had to start slowly, giving her clear liquids first, then soft foods. Her eyes lit up when, after a day of Pedialyte and juice, she saw me open a jar of applesauce. She loved the first bite. But it wasn't enough. She wanted more—and more. She pulled at the spoon and cried when I had to call a halt to the meal.

Paul's hunger to know Jesus more and more drove him to act. First, he clearly defined his goal: to "gain Christ and be completely united with him" (Phil. 3:8-9 TEV); "to know Christ and to experience the power of his resurrection, to share in his sufferings and become like him in his death" (Phil. 3:10 TEV).

Then, having stated his aim, Paul relentlessly pursued it. Twice in verses 12-14 he said, "I press on" (NIV). Like a runner in a footrace, he surged forward, focusing all his energies on reaching his desired end.

Recall a time you were really thirsty. Your whole body screamed for water. You looked for a way to quench your thirst, and when you finally found it—what did you do? Take just a sip or two? Or drink long and deeply?

Mary, like Paul, wanted to know Jesus. When He came to visit, she didn't just walk through the room and call out a quick "Hi." She stopped, humbled herself before Him, and listened. For a time, she laid other things—important things—aside. She drank deeply of His teachings.

Through listening, she came to know her Teacher. She likely heard Him speak truths He could not entrust to the masses. She began to understand what moved Him, what angered Him, what hurt Him, what pleased Him. She gained new insight into the God-nature of the Man at whose feet she sat. She came to know His ways.

Perhaps her heart echoed the prayer Moses had

11

prayed hundreds of years earlier: "If I have found favor in your eyes, teach me your ways so I may know you and continue to find favor with you" (Ex. 33:13 NIV).

What about you? Do you hunger for Christ so much that other things have lost their significance? Do you yearn to gain a deeper relationship with Him every day? Do you put aside other matters to spend time getting to know Him better?

Your new heart has the capacity to hunger and thirst for Christ. Cultivate that capacity. Develop an appetite for intimacy with God. Then, claim the promise His Word holds out to the hungry of heart: "He satisfies those who are thirsty and fills the hungry with good things" (Psalm 107:8 TEV).

REPROGRAM Read aloud 2 Timothy 2:21 three times. Begin memorizing this verse.

RESPOND Ask God to develop in you the same hunger to know Him that Mary and Paul had. Thank Him that He will not only create that hunger, but also satisfy it.

D A Y   5

WHO AM I?

I am a woman with a hungry heart: I yearn for God to use me

Which person would seem to you a more likely candidate for God to use: a young refugee widow from a pagan nation, or a supernaturally strong Hebrew leader separated to God from birth?

Ruth (the refugee widow) and Samson (the strong Hebrew) lived during the days of Israel's judges. Neither was perfect. But both were used by God. Ruth, however—the less likely—was used more fully.

READ Ruth 2:2-12; Judges 16:18-20. List character traits of Ruth and Samson that these two passages reveal.

REFLECT Ruth had a heart hungry to please God. As a result, the Lord used her to bless her mother-in-law, Naomi, and to give birth to Obed, grandfather of David, forefather of Jesus.

Samson sought to please himself. He either broke his Nazarite vow or walked right to the edge of it 20 years before Delilah cut his hair, when he touched a lion's carcass (Judg. 14:5-9; Num. 6:6). Three times, he entered into forbidden relationships with Philistine women (Judg. 14:1-2; 16:1,4; Ex. 34:12-16).

For 20 years God, in His grace, used Samson. At the end of those two decades, however, Samson fell—dragging the Lord's name down with him. Whereas Ruth's story ended in victory, Samson's ended in tragedy.

13

Many years after Ruth and Samson lived, the apostle Paul wrote: "If anyone makes himself clean from all those evil things, he will be used for special purposes, because he is dedicated and useful to his Master, ready to be used for every good deed" (2 Tim. 2:21 TEV).

Do you yearn to be used by God "for special purposes"? Do you want Him to use you, not in spite of yourself, but because you are "dedicated and useful" to Him? Yes? Ah. Your new heart is hungry. To satisfy that hunger, try taking these steps:

1. PREPARE YOURSELF. Don't harbor sin for days, months, or even years, as Samson did. Instead, confess and forsake "all those evil things."

What evil things? "What is ignoble and unclean . . . contaminating and corrupting influences" (2 Tim. 2:21 Amplified). Five verses earlier, Paul had warned against "godless chatter," asserting "those who indulge in it will become more and more ungodly" (2 Tim. 2:16 NIV).

2. PRESENT YOURSELF. Do what 2 Timothy 2:15 advises: "Be diligent to present yourself approved to God as a workman who does not need to be ashamed, handling accurately the word of truth" (NASB).

"Be diligent to present yourself. . . ." Arriving in a strange land, knowing no one, Ruth didn't sit around waiting for others to take the initiative. Instead, she begged Naomi, "Let me go to the fields" (Ruth 2:2 TEV).

If you hunger to be useful to God, step forward eagerly, like a soldier volunteering for a mission. Have as your constant attitude before God, "Here am I. Send me."

"Approved to God." By first seeking her mother-in-law's counsel, then asking permission from the one in charge of the field in which she wanted to glean, Ruth let God guide her (Ruth 2:2,5-7).

You, too, should "Do your best to win full approval in God's sight" (2 Tim. 2:15 TEV). Be ready to work—but await God's go-ahead. Seek His instructions.

"A workman who does not need to be ashamed." Ruth began gleaning early one morning. Stopping only for a rest break and lunch, she worked until evening (Ruth 2:7,14,17). The next day, she was back—and the next, and the next. In fact, Ruth continued to glean until the

14

end, not only of the barley harvest, but also of the wheat harvest (Ruth 2:23). Her industriousness caused both Boaz and Naomi to praise the Lord (Ruth 2:12,20).

When you accept a task, see it through to completion. Don't fizzle. Don't piddle. Rather, let your attitude be that expressed by Paul in Philippians 1:20: "My deep desire and hope is that I shall never fail in my duty, but that at all times, and especially right now, I shall be full of courage, so that with my whole being I shall bring honor to Christ" (TEV).

"Handling accurately the word of truth." God's Word provided a way for a childless widow in Israel to have a kinsman-redeemer (Deut. 25:5-10). Guided by Naomi, Ruth received God's provision (Ruth 3-4).

If you are to be used most fully by God, learn how to handle His Word correctly. Seek to know the Bible a little better each day. Ask the Holy Spirit to teach you which truths, which commands, which promises, apply in situations you encounter.

As you prepare yourself and present yourself, God will satisfy your hunger to be used for special purposes.

REPROGRAM Finish memorizing 2 Timothy 2:21. Repeat Ephesians 2:10.

RESPOND Jot down ways God is using you. Is He doing so because you are fit for His use—or in spite of the fact that you are not fit? Ask Him to show you one thing you can do to be more fit for Him.

D A Y   6

WHO AM I?

I am a woman with a sensitive heart: I see others' needs

Jesus never met a need He didn't recognize. In Nicodemus, He saw a teacher needing to be taught (John 3). In a crowd of disabled persons, He spotted a lame man wanting to get well (John 5). Jesus saw that the 5,000 needed not only food, but also straight talk about the Bread of Life (John 6). He realized that an adulterous woman needed forgiveness (John 8).

Even when tired, hot, and hungry, Jesus recognized the deepest needs of a Samaritan woman—a person most other Jews would not have even noticed.

READ John 4:5-26. Jot down what the woman thought her needs were. Write what Jesus knew her needs to be.

REFLECT It was noon. The Traveler had already walked many miles. Sitting beside a well, He waited for food. The heat lulled Him. Dust covered Him.

Squinting in the overhead sun, He watched a woman make her way toward the well. He might easily have ignored her. She didn't expect Him to speak.

But He did speak. He could not ignore what His sensitive heart saw.

Warning, Christian: the sensitive heart of Jesus beats within you. His heart makes you alert to things you normally would not see. His sensitivity functions even in a weary body. It can enable you to see past your own needs to the needs of others. . . .

You've had a hard day. The children haven't minded. The air conditioner's gone out. Your husband walks in the door just as the potatoes boil over. Did you notice his stooped shoulders? Did you hear the discouraged edge to his voice? Or were you so busy giving vent to your frustrations that you never thought to inquire, "What's wrong, hon?"

It's final exam week. You have been hitting the books so hard you see pages in your sleep. You face your hardest exam tomorrow morning. Opening a soft drink, you settle in for an intense study session. Do you notice your non-Christian roomie doodling absent-mindedly on her paper? Do you pay any attention when she walks to the window and stares out? Does it occur to you to ask, "Hey, roomie, want to talk?"

You're late for an important meeting. Turning a corner, you see your destination. Do you also see the elderly woman walking down the street struggling to carry a bag of groceries?

Putting His own needs aside, Jesus observed the Samaritan woman. He saw not only her perceived needs, but also her unperceived ones.

Obviously, she needed water. Jesus talked to her first about water. Then, He guided the conversation around to her deepest need, the need to know Him as her Lord and Saviour.

His sensitive heart within you can read other hearts. It can enable you to see beyond superficial needs to hidden ones . . .

You and your family are moving—or trying to move. Your preschooler is taking things out of boxes faster than you can put them in. You have already scolded and taken away privileges and even spanked. You are on the verge of spanking again when you realize what's happening. Your child is bewildered. He needs to know that, in all this turmoil, your love for him holds firm. His belligerence is the only way he knows to express his need.

Your next-door neighbor has a retriever puppy. The puppy has retrieved your newspaper, your boots, and several other things you forgot to anchor down. When you politely asked your neighbor to restrain her dog, she lashed out at you. You are thinking of calling the city pound when you realize how little you've seen the woman's husband at home lately. You recall several incidents that make you wonder whether the woman's angry remarks were expressions of her frustration over a failing marriage. You pick up the phone, but instead of calling the pound, you call your neighbor—and invite her over for coffee.

You are watching the evening news. The anchorperson begins an account of another outbreak of violence in the Middle East. You have heard such stories before. About to change channels, you catch the faces of several persons involved in the conflict. Suddenly, you *see* them. You see real people trying to live through war. You know that the vast majority of those people do not know Christ. Immediately, you stop and pray.

Yes, Christian, you have Jesus' sensitive heart. But you may or may not be cultivating that sensitivity.

The determining factor is focus. If you are constantly preoccupied with yourself—*your* plans, *your* problems, *your* responsibilities—you won't observe others. As you commit your goals and needs to God, and trust Him to handle them, your mind and heart are freed to turn outward. Then, when persons in need cross your path, Christ in you enables you to see.

REPROGRAM   Repeat from memory 2 Timothy 2:21 and Ephesians 2:10.

RESPOND   List persons with whom you came in contact yesterday. What needs might they have been trying to communicate that you failed to see? Ask God to show you someone's hidden need today.

WHO AM I?

I am a woman with a sensitive heart: I hurt when others hurt

Jesus' friend Lazarus lay dying. Jesus could have healed him. He could have spoken from the far side of Jordan, and, over in Bethany, Lazarus would have been made well. But Jesus had better plans.

He waited two days. Then He journeyed to Bethany, knowing Lazarus was dead. As the Lord approached the village where his friend's body lay, first Martha, then Mary came out to meet Him. With Mary came a large crowd of mourners. Jesus' response to the bereaved sisters showed the depths of His sensitive heart perhaps more than at any other time.

READ   John 11:32-44. Mark words and phrases that indicate Jesus' feelings.

REFLECT   Jesus was deeply moved when He saw Mary's and Martha's grief. Why? Did He not know their story would have a happy ending? Certainly, He knew the miracle He was about to do. He knew the sisters' sorrow would turn to joy. He had waited and He had come because He loved them, because He wanted to see their faith strengthened and God glorified.

Why, then, was He so deeply moved that He wept? His sensitive heart felt Martha's and Mary's pain. Knowing they would rejoice with Him later, He cried with them at the moment of their grief.

The new heart Jesus created in you is vulnerable to

19

pain. It's sensitive. That does not mean it is easily offended or hurt by personal wrongs you may suffer. Jesus
didn't get huffy and leave when both Mary and Martha
scolded Him for not coming sooner.

Rather, your new heart in Christ beats with godly
love, the love that "does not keep a record of wrongs"
(1 Cor. 13:5 TEV). Because of that love, you can shrug
off insults to yourself. You can feel deeply the hurts of
others. You can "weep with those who weep" (Rom.
12:15 TEV).

Ouch. That hurts.

Yes, it's frightening and, at times, painful to carry a
sensitive heart into a cruel world. It is much safer to
build protective walls around your heart and to call to
hurting ones from behind those walls, "It'll be all right."

But God's love risks openness. "If a rich person sees
his brother in need, yet closes his heart against his
brother, how can he claim that he loves God?" (1 John
3:17 TEV).

God's love risks involvement. Twice in the Lazarus
story, John noted that Jesus was "deeply moved" (vv.
33, 38). John also recorded, "his heart was touched" (v.
33). The Greek word translated *deeply moved* contains an
element of anger, as a horse might express by snorting.
"His heart was touched" can also be rendered, "His
heart was agitated, like a pool of water."

Moved by compassion, Jesus chafed to ease the hurt
Mary and Martha felt. He quietly but publicly shed tears
with the sisters. Then, in love and wisdom, He acted.
He brought Lazarus back to life. Later, by His own death
and resurrection, He conquered death for His friends—
and for every sufferer who has ever lived.

You can develop the sensitive heart you've been given
in Christ if you will obey God's command to open yourself to risk. "As those who have been chosen of God,
holy and beloved, put on a heart of compassion" (Col.
3:12 NASB).

Remember, you received "a heart of compassion"
when you received Christ as Saviour. Moment by moment you choose whether to put it on.

Right now, visualize yourself taking off your old, cold
heart. Picture yourself putting on your new, caring one.

Then, when you don't *feel* like weeping with those who weep, choose to do so. When you would rather *not* shoulder someone else's burden, gladly do it anyway.

Let the hurt, the agitation, the disquiet you feel for others move you toward action. Through your tears, seek solutions.

Jesus said, "Happy are those who mourn" (Matt. 5:4 TEV). In so saying, He pronounced a blessing, not only on those who sorrow over their own sins and griefs, but also on those who sorrow over the sins and griefs of others. He promised all who hurt in behalf of others special comfort and joy.

About three years after speaking that blessing, Jesus Himself experienced the fulness of its truth. He bore the ultimate hurt on our behalf—death on a cross—knowing that on the other side of that great hurt lay a greater joy (Heb. 12:2).

Don't protect your sensitive heart. Receive it as evidence that you are in Christ. Put it on as part of your spiritual growth process. Let inner turmoil over the pains of others pave the way for outward, God-glorifying action. In so doing, you will "know Him, and the power of His resurrection and the fellowship of His sufferings" (Phil. 3:10 NASB). In so doing, you will receive His blessing.

REPROGRAM Begin memorizing Colossians 3:12.

RESPOND Which hurts in those around you, as well as in the world, have deeply moved you lately? Picture yourself opening your heart to others' hurts. Tell God your willingness to weep with those who weep. Claim the promise of Matthew 5:4.

DAY 8

WHO AM I?

I am a woman with a hearing heart: I recognize God's voice

Once you begin to see and feel others' needs, you may think that you personally must solve them all. But though God wants you to weep and pray over the world's hurts, He does not want you to act until He gives the go-ahead. Consequently, He has equipped your new heart with ears to hear His call.

READ 1 Samuel 3:1-10; 16:1-3,10-13. Contrast Samuel's ability to recognize God's voice in the two chapters.

REFLECT Have you ever heard God's voice? If you are His child, you have. With the ears of your heart, you heard His call to salvation.

Perhaps you, like Samuel, had trouble recognizing that first call as the voice of the Lord. Maybe you considered the inner prompting of God's Spirit a "feeling." Maybe you wanted to respond, but did not know how. Maybe you sought out a Christian who could help you understand that God was the One tugging at your spirit, that He was calling you to receive Jesus Christ as your Lord.

Regardless of the circumstances, you started out, as Samuel did, not knowing the Lord, not previously having heard His voice. You received a hearing heart when you said yes to Jesus.

Most likely, you will never hear God speak to you audibly. Yet, using the following principles, you can train the ears of your heart to better recognize God's voice.

1. PUT YOURSELF IN GOD'S PRESENCE. God spoke as Samuel lay "in the temple of the Lord where the ark of God was" (1 Sam. 3:3 NASB). In the Old Testament, the ark symbolized God's presence.

God the Holy Spirit has lived in you since the day of your conversion. To make His presence real to you at any given moment, simply claim the promise that He is there. Say, for example, "Thank You, Spirit of truth, that You remain with me and live in me" (based on John 14:16-17). Try to grasp the fact that the God of the universe stands ready to speak a word in your ear.

Learn to invoke God's presence through praise. As you confess who He is and what He has done, He who "inhabitest the praises of Israel" (Psalm 22:3 KJV) will make His presence known.

2. INVITE HIM TO SPEAK. Like Samuel, you can say, "Speak, Lord, your servant is listening" (1 Sam. 3:9 TEV). When seeking God's will about a specific need, name the need. Ask, "Lord, what is Your will regarding . . . ? What would you have me do?" Ask Him to make His answer very clear.

3. WAIT AND LISTEN. After Samuel learned that the voice he had heard was the Lord's, he went back to bed (v. 3:9). Do you think he slept? More likely, he waited, wide-eyed, for God Almighty to speak again.

As you daily, systematically read the Bible, expect one or more of the verses to produce a quickening within you. Receive that quickening as God's voice directing, encouraging, convicting, or teaching you. If no quickening comes, linger over the verses. Reread them. If you still don't hear the Spirit's quiet voice, tell God you are continuing to listen, and go on about the tasks of the day.

God will choose the time to answer. He may speak another day as you read your Bible. He may bring a Scripture verse to mind while you are doing something else altogether. He may nudge you during Sunday School, a BYW meeting, or a worship service. Don't be surprised if He speaks at a totally unexpected time— perhaps even in the middle of the night.

When you believe you have His answer, make sure the impression in your spirit coincides with the clear commands of the Word. Don't accept as from the Lord anything that contradicts Scripture.

4. IF YOU THINK YOU HAVE HEARD FROM HIM, but are unclear about it, ask Him to explain or confirm His leading. When God told Samuel to anoint a new king, the prophet first asked, "How?" (1 Sam. 16:2). God told him how, but He didn't tell Samuel *who* until the moment David entered the room.

Don't hesitate to ask God for further guidance when you need it, but remember: the Lord reserves the right to explain only as much as He chooses. Many times, He will tell you just what you need to know to take the next step. Only when you have taken that step will He reveal more.

5. WHATEVER HE TELLS YOU, DO IT. God told Samuel to go to Bethlehem. "Samuel did what the Lord told him" (16:4 TEV). Then, Samuel refused to anoint anyone until God declared, "This is the one" (16:12 TEV).

If you hear God speak yet you do not obey, He is not likely to speak again (except to reiterate what He has told you). Disobedience invites God's silence.

You have a hearing heart. You have a speaking God. The two will connect as you learn to listen.

REPROGRAM Finish memorizing Colossians 3:12. Repeat 2 Timothy 2:21.

RESPOND Ask God to show you one need in another person's life that He wants you to act on. Ask Him what first step He wants you to take. When He speaks, record His answer.

D A Y 9

WHO AM I?

I am a woman with a hearing heart: I respond when God calls

Little did Rebecca know, when she took up her waterpot that evening, how drastically her life was about to change. Approaching the well, she noticed a stranger and ten heavily-loaded camels kneeling beside him. He did not speak. She filled her jar in silence. As she turned to go, however, the man hurried toward her.

"Please give me a little water from your jar."

"Drink, sir. I will draw water for your camels, too." Running back and forth from well to trough, she finished the task for which she had volunteered.

"Whose daughter are you?" asked the stranger.

Before Rebecca knew what was happening, the man was standing in her home, explaining his mission to her family.

READ Genesis 24:47-58. List reasons Rebecca might have chosen not to go with Abraham's servant.

REFLECT Put yourself in Rebecca's place: Yesterday, you showed kindness to a stranger. Now, he is asking you to travel with him to a faraway country. If you go, you will be leaving your family and homeland forever. Upon reaching your destination, you will marry a man you have never met.

You don't have a month—or even a week—to make your decision, get things in order, pack, and say your good-byes. The stranger wants to leave today.

25

Will you go with him?

Rebecca could have said no. Although her family had given their initial OK, she alone had to make the final decision. Picture it: The question, "Will you go with this man?" hung in the air. Rebecca looked at Mama, Daddy, and brother Laban, knowing they wanted her to balk. She looked at the stranger and tried to imagine the unseen father and son he represented. With her whole life hanging in the balance she said, "I will go" (v. 58 NIV).

One day, probably when you were least expecting it, the Holy Spirit came to you with an even bolder offer. On behalf of God the Father, He invited you to receive Christ and so become part of the Church, the Bride of God's Son. Like Rebecca, you had to make your decision without ever having seen your Groom.

Also like Rebecca, you could have said no. You may not have realized it at the time, but when you said yes, you made a radical decision. Your life took a different course.

During your Christian pilgrimage, the Lord has issued other invitations to you. He has called you to serve in His church in one or more capacities. (At different times, He has probably called you into different avenues of service.)

He has called you to follow Him in making such life choices as which college to attend, what career to pursue, and whether to marry.

He has called you to give witness of Him to those with whom you come in contact. He has called you to show by your life the reality that God dwells within.

Further, He has called you to be separated from the world, yet vitally involved in it.

If you have responded to God's past calls, you may be tempted to sit back and relax. Please, don't get too comfortable. God's people, like medical interns, are always on call.

Both Isaiah and Jonah had said yes to God's call to prophesy. Then God spoke to each man again. The Lord called Isaiah to proclaim a special message (Isa. 6:1-10). The Lord commanded Jonah to go to a special place (Jonah 1:1-3).

26

Isaiah immediately followed the leading of his hearing heart. With the words, "I will go! Send me!" (Isa. 6:8 TEV), he readily accepted a difficult, less-than-desirable mission. Jonah "ran away from the Lord" (Jonah 1:3 NIV). Only after causing himself and his shipmates great distress did he obey God.

Rebecca's family gave yet another type of response. They said yes, then no. Initially, they agreed to let their daughter go with Abraham's servant. But when the time came for her to leave, they said, "Wait."

What about you? What is your Lord asking of you today? What are you answering?

Your new heart, your hearing heart, wants to say yes. Are you following its prompting? Or are you resisting? Are you trying to run from something you know the Lord wants you to do? Or are you, perhaps, trying to stall for time?

To a would-be disciple who said, " 'I will follow you, Lord; but first let me go back and say good-bye to my family,' Jesus replied, 'No one who puts his hand to the plow and looks back is fit for service in the kingdom of God' " (Luke 9:61-62 NIV).

When Jesus calls, lay aside your reservations and go.

REPROGRAM Repeat from memory Colossians 3:12 and 2 Timothy 2:21.

RESPOND Commit yourself to take the action God indicated as you prayed yesterday. Sometime today: (1) tell a Christian friend of your commitment and ask to be held accountable; (2) take a first step toward doing what God has called you to do.

D A Y   1 0

WHO AM I?

I am a woman with a wholly committed heart

Remember Solomon? He got rave reviews in the Old Testament. In fact, he was so highly touted that the Queen of Sheba scoffed—until she came to Jerusalem to see for herself. Then she testified, "What I heard in my own country about you and your wisdom is true! . . . But I didn't hear even half of it; your wisdom and wealth are much greater than what I was told" (1 Kings 10:6-7 TEV).

Yet, in the New Testament, Solomon doesn't fare well at all. He is not listed in the Hebrews 11 roll call of the faithful. He is not often quoted, as is his father, David. He is mentioned only twice by the Lord Jesus. Once, Jesus compared Solomon's clothing to that of the lilies (the lilies are better clothed). Another time, Christ compared Solomon's wisdom to His own (Jesus is far wiser).

So what happened to Solomon?

He suffered heart failure.

READ 1 Kings 2:1-4; 11:1-4. Contrast the heart condition God requires with the heart condition Solomon developed.

REFLECT Elderly King David stood his son Solomon in front of all the officials of Israel and gave the young heir to the throne this solemn charge: "My son, I charge you to acknowledge your father's God and to serve him with an undivided heart and a willing mind" (1 Chron. 28:9 TEV).

Solomon took his father's charge seriously—at first.

He prayed for wisdom, rather than riches. He built Israel's temple, just as God had commanded. He ruled a kingdom marked by peace and plenty.

But while Solomon was busy doing things for God and God's people, he failed to take his own good advice: he failed to "watch over [his] heart with all diligence" (Prov. 4:23 NASB).

Instead of making sure that his whole heart continued to belong to God, he gave his heart, piece by piece, to idolatrous women and the gods they worshiped.

As a result, Solomon lost the kingdom of Israel (1 Kings 11:9-13). He lost all purpose and joy in life (Eccl. 1:1-2). He lost his witness. The author of 1 Kings records, "His heart was not wholly devoted to the Lord his God, as the heart of David his father had been" (v. 11:4 NASB).

Don't think, It couldn't happen to me. The members of the church in Ephesus probably thought that, too. They had worked hard for Christ. They had taken a firm stand against false apostles. They had persevered under trial. Yet when Jesus sent the Ephesian believers a letter, He said, "You do not love me now as you did at first" (Rev. 2:4 TEV). Their hearts no longer fully belonged to their Lord.

Every Christian possesses a new heart. That heart has been created in Christ Jesus. It is being perfected by the Lord. It is a heart:
• hungry to know God and to be used by Him
• sensitive to the needs of those who hurt
• alert and responsive to God's call.

Do you see these qualities in yourself? They may not be full-blown. They will need nurturing. But the qualities are there if the new heart is. If you do not see them, either you have never received Christ or you have tried to reclaim a part of your heart.

The first commandment, the most important one, applies to you today just as much as it did to the Israelites to whom God first gave it: "Love the Lord your God with all your heart, with all your soul, with all your mind, and with all your strength" (Mark 12:30 TEV).

In obeying that commandment, you gain power to obey the others. "For the eyes of the Lord move to and fro throughout the earth that He may strongly support those whose heart is completely His" (2 Chron. 16:9a NASB).

Picture it: God is looking earthward. His eyes scan the globe. Then, for a moment, He pauses, focusing on you. He looks, not *at* you, but *into* you. What does he see? Does he see a heart fully focused on Him?

Corrie ten Boom once used a glass of water to explain the heart wholly turned toward God. First, she held the glass upside down. Obviously, it held no water. Then she tilted the glass at different angles. Only when the glass was perfectly upright could it be filled.

Only when your heart is fully upright toward God can you be filled with His Spirit. Only then can you claim the power of His strong support.

Are you watching over your heart "with all diligence"? If not, it may tilt ever so slightly, then more, and more, away from God. If, however, you will constantly choose to love the Lord with all your heart, you will be, in ever increasing measure, spiritually hungry, sensitive, willing to hear, and able to obey God.

REPROGRAM Say aloud Colossians 3:12; 2 Timothy 2:21; Ephesians 2:10. Ponder each verse as you say it.

RESPOND Pray a prayer of thanksgiving based on the devotions for days 1 through 10. Begin, "Thank You, Lord that through You I am. . . ." After giving thanks, offer your whole heart afresh to God.

D A Y 1 1

WHO ARE WE?

We're women

Our pastor had preached a powerful sermon. As the invitation hymn began, one woman, then another stepped down from the choir to pray at the altar. Each wept quietly as she prayed. A woman and a teenage girl left the balcony together. They too knelt at the altar. A woman from the congregation made her way to the pastor and whispered her decision to him.

The Spirit had moved. Who had responded?

Women.

READ Luke 7:36-50. Contrast the actions and attitudes of the unnamed woman with those of Simon and the others at the table with Jesus.

REFLECT A woman dared to enter Simon's dinner party uninvited. Although bystanders could come to such gatherings in Jesus' day, this woman would hardly have been welcome. The host was a Pharisee, religiously above reproach. The woman had "lived a sinful life" (v. 37 TEV). She was probably a prostitute.

She stopped behind Jesus, who was reclining on a couch provided for dinner guests, and she cried. She cried so much she had to use her hair as a towel to wipe Jesus' feet. Simon was offended, but Jesus was not. He understood the reasons for her tears.

1. SHE WEPT TO EXPRESS REPENTANCE. When Jesus said to the woman, "Your sins are forgiven" (v. 48 TEV), she did not draw back and retort, "What sins?" She attempted no cover-ups, offered no excuses. By her presence, her demeanor, her silence, she admitted, "I have done great wrong."

31

If Jesus had made the same remark to Simon, the Pharisee would probably have been indignant. He saw no sins in himself. Yet, during that one dinner, he showed inhospitality, self-righteousness, and pride.

Like Simon, we can often point instantly to wrongdoing in others. Like him, we are often able to ignore or rationalize even the most glaring sins in ourselves.

Jesus saw in Simon unconfessed wrongs—and rebuked him. Jesus saw in the woman the sorrow that leads to repentance (2 Cor. 7:10)—and commended her.

2. SHE WEPT TO EXPRESS FAITH. At the end of the encounter at the dinner party, Jesus told the woman, "Your faith has saved you; go in peace" (v. 50 TEV).

She did not say aloud, "Lord Jesus, I believe in you." Yet, He knew that faith had prompted her to choose a gift of expensive perfume with which to anoint Him. Faith had propelled her to seek Him out, regardless of the cost.

Once she stood directly behind Jesus, with opportunity to express what she believed, only tears had come. Jesus recognized in those tears her confession of faith in Him.

The other dinner guests questioned Jesus' authority to forgive sins. The woman believed not only that He could forgive sins, but that He would forgive *her* sins.

3. SHE WEPT TO EXPRESS LOVE. Jesus said to Simon, "The great love she has shown proves that her many sins have been forgiven" (v. 47 TEV).

Even before Jesus spoke forgiveness to the woman (v. 48), He had given it—and she had received it. Perhaps the transaction took place when she stooped to wipe her tears from His feet. Perhaps she knew that, in allowing her to touch Him, He had declared her clean.

Whatever the timing, the woman suddenly realized she had been forgiven, and a new love for Jesus overpowered her. Continuing to cry, she kept wiping Jesus' feet with her hair, kissing His feet, and pouring perfume on them. Not caring who looked on, she lavished her love on the Lord Jesus. Yet, bowing herself to touch only His feet, she showed utter humility, respect, and submission.

In contrast, Simon apparently never touched Jesus.

He did not greet his guest with a kiss on the cheek, wash his feet, or anoint his head—all common courtesies of the day. Throughout the dinner, Simon remained aloof, in body, soul, and spirit. Unwilling to give himself to Christ, He failed to receive all that Jesus could have given him in return.

As women, we must be careful not to let our emotions control us. By following our emotions, we may be led astray. By seeking emotional experiences, we may miss true worship.

Yet, let us unashamedly express our God-given emotions in God-pleasing ways. Let us be bold to express grief over sin, faith in Christ, and love for Him—with tears, if tears should come. Others may think us foolish. Jesus will commend us and send us away in peace.

He is worthy.

REPROGRAM Read 1 Peter 2:9-10 aloud several times. Memorize verse 9.

RESPOND Are you embarrassed to express your love for Jesus with tears? Thank God that He made you a woman. Spend a few minutes naming specific things Jesus has done for you. Then, spend a few minutes worshiping Him unashamedly.

DAY 12

WHO ARE WE?

We're women who know

Insecure. Uncertain. These words describe many women today. Such women don't know what, or whom, to believe. They live with fear and worry. If nothing changes, "like a high wall with a crack running down it; suddenly [they] will collapse" (Isa. 30:13 TEV).

One Sunday morning nearly 2,000 years ago, several women walked toward a grave. They, too, were insecure and uncertain—until they reached an empty tomb.

READ Luke 24:1-11. Jot down adjectives that describe the women's state of mind (a) before they reached the tomb, and (b) after leaving the tomb.

REFLECT The women who walked toward Jesus' tomb had believed in Him. During His earthly ministry, they had followed Him, served Him, loved Him. They intended to minister to Him one last time by anointing His body. Their mission was one of love, but one without hope or power. If Jesus had been in that grave, their anointing Him would have changed nothing.

The women who ran from Jesus' tomb had a new mission—a mission both of hope and power. They went immediately to tell the disciples the good news, "Jesus is alive!" Yet, the Lord's closest followers refused to believe them.

What did the women do then? Cry? Fume? Throw things? Begin to doubt what they had seen and heard?

We are not told that they made *any* response. No longer insecure or uncertain, they had confidence. They were now women who knew.

What had happened? They had followed God's orders

34

for those who find themselves "like a high wall with a crack running down it." The orders? "Come back and quietly trust in me. Then you will be strong and secure" (Isa. 30:15 TEV).

1. COME BACK. The women may have gone to the tomb for the wrong reason, but at least they went to the tomb. They made their way to the place they believed their Lord to be.

When we find our world turned upside down, we may want to act like my newborn daughter did when her stomach hurt. She cried, of course. And as I walked her and tried to comfort her, she pounded on my shoulder with her tiny fists.

We may sometimes feel like pounding on God's shoulder, little realizing that He is the One holding us up, offering us comfort. But when we have finished our moment of protest, let us come back to the One who is faithful. Let us rest in His arms. As we do, He will restore our confidence.

"God is our shelter and strength, always ready to
    help in times of trouble.
So we will not be afraid, even if the earth is shaken
    and the mountains fall into the ocean depths."
        (Psalm 46:1-2 TEV)

2. QUIETLY TRUST. The disciples thought the women's claims regarding Jesus were nonsense. But though their tale seemed impossible and though other followers of Christ scoffed, the women knew Jesus was alive. They quietly trusted Him to prove them right.

What happened at the tomb that gave them such confidence?

They remembered His words. The angels had urged them: "Remember what he said to you while he was in Galilee" (Luke 24:6 TEV). He had said He would die on a cross. He had said He would rise again.

Before seeing the empty tomb, the women had forgotten their Lord's promise of resurrection. When they remembered His words, they began to regain their confidence.

They received His messengers. Recognizing that the two men who stood inside the tomb were, indeed, God's messengers, the women accepted the message: "He is

35

not here; he has risen!" (v. 6 NIV). They headed out to tell others what they had heard, certain that He who had spoken was faithful.

They reverenced their Lord. Matthew records that, as the women were on their way, "Suddenly Jesus met them and said, 'Peace be with you.' They came up to him, took hold of his feet, and worshiped him" (Matt. 28:9 TEV). In His presence, their confidence was fully restored.

Like the women at the tomb, we are women who know. We know the God who is faithful. We know that His Word is true. We know that God has passed down to us the mission of hope and power first given to those who viewed the empty tomb: Remember! (Luke 24:6); tell! (Matt. 28:7).

Sometimes our confidence may falter. Our walls may develop cracks. When that happens, let's make them strong and secure again. Let's come back to our Lord. Let's quietly trust His words—even when others (some of whom should know better) scoff.

REPROGRAM Finish memorizing 1 Peter 2:9-10. Repeat Ephesians 2:10.

RESPOND Identify a promise or assurance God has given—but you have failed to remember or claim. Meditate on Isaiah 30:15. Praise God for His faithfulness. Determine to stand firm on His true word.

D A Y   1 3

WHO ARE WE?

We're women who know who we are

We are his people, we are his flock" (Psalm 100:3 TEV). The psalmist wrote those words about Israel, a nation with traceable bloodlines, distinct features, geographical boundaries.

"At one time you were not God's people, but now you are his people" (1 Peter 2:10 TEV). Peter is referring to believers. Unlike the Jews, we who formerly "were not God's people" might, at first glance, seem to have little in common. But, looking at 1 Peter 2, we begin to see the many common bonds we Christians have.

READ   1 Peter 2:4-10. Mark terms Peter used to identify believers.

REFLECT   We are Christians. Peter called us "you that believe" (v. 7 TEV). As "living stones" (v. 5 TEV), we are each individual. We are each chosen by God and precious to Him.

But just as a house is more than a pile of uncut stones, we are more than a collection of individuals. God is building us, His people, into a "spiritual temple" (v. 5). That requires shaping and wise placing. Sometimes, both make us uncomfortable. Sometimes, we may feel we don't "fit" where God is trying to put us.

Recently, my husband and I bought a house that was under construction. Stacks of multicolored bricks cluttered the yard. Looking at those bricks, I saw hues and shades that seemed to clash. After the bricks were laid, however, I took another look. All the bricks blended

37

well. The bricklayer had put each in the right place to bring out its own beauty, as well as the beauty of the work around it.

The walls of our house testify to the skill of the bricklayer. The walls of God's spiritual temple testify to His power to create a people from those who were "not God's people."

1. WE ARE MANY COLORS—yet God has made us one race. One race? It would be impossible to pick members of "the chosen race" (v. 9) out of a line-up, based on outward appearance. We have differing physical features, as well as differing personalities and backgrounds. We are not visibly related. But we are kin. We have one Father.

2. WE ARE FROM MANY COUNTRIES—yet God has made us one nation. Those from the United States can say the pledge of allegiance with pride. Those from other countries can take equal delight in their nationalities. But we all have a higher allegiance. We are citizens of a different kingdom.

No mapmaker can chart our kingdom's boundaries. No road signs mark them. But all of us who have received Jesus as Lord have passed the same invisible marker. It reads: "Welcome! You have just entered God's kingdom."

3. WE HAVE MANY OCCUPATIONS—yet we are all priests. Some of us manage the home full time. Others are students. Many have careers outside the home. A multitude of jobs demand our time and attention. Yet God has given to all of us a common job assignment. We are to offer service to Him. We are to approach Him in behalf of others.

In the Old Testament, God chose the men of one Israelite tribe to receive the priesthood. Those men offered sacrifices on the people's behalf. In Christ, the old sacrifices and the old priesthood were superseded. Now, God gives each Christian the privilege of offering "spiritual and acceptable sacrifices to God through Jesus Christ" (v. 5 TEV). As "the King's priests" (1 Peter 2:9 TEV), we are all responsible to offer our bodies (Rom. 12:1), our possessions (Phil. 4:18), and our words and our deeds (Heb. 13:15-16) to Him.

4. WE MAY SEEM A MOTLEY CREW—yet we are God's special treasure. Not many of us are wise (as the world views wisdom); not many, rich; not many, corporate heads; not many, movie stars. Most of us will never find our names in *Who's Who*. Yet the God who owns all the universe, who rules all the peoples, has designated *us* His special treasure.

One stone can be used in a few ways; many stones can be used in a multitude of ways. God chose us as His race, His nation, His priests, His treasure *to proclaim His wonderful acts*. Each of us can proclaim Him in a few ways. All of us together can proclaim Him in a multitude of ways.

So He places us, one against another and another and another, that together we may "declare the praises of him who called [us] out of darkness into his wonderful light" (1 Peter 2:9 NIV).

Let us cooperate in the shaping and fitting-together process. In so doing, we show that we know who we are. In so doing, we show that we know *whose* we are.

REPROGRAM Repeat 1 Peter 2:9-10 twice from memory. Review Colossians 3:12.

RESPOND Is there any one of God's people whom you'd object to being put next to in God's "spiritual temple"? Is there any Baptist Young Woman with whom you've had trouble relating? Confess these attitude problems. Ask God to make you aware—and repentant—any time you hinder His "building together" process.

D A Y   1 4

WHO ARE WE?

We're women who know who we are in Christ

Where we are affects who we are. Young women who go away to college change. In a new setting out from under parental wing, they may show new maturity and responsibility or they may rebel. Either way, they change.

Women who relocate because of their own or their husbands' jobs tend to develop different life-styles and buying habits. They may drop out of church—or become more active. They may withdraw socially—or make new friends.

Spiritually, where we are determines who we are. We who believe in the Lord Jesus are in the safest, most blessed place in all creation. We are *in Christ*.

READ Ephesians 1:3-14. Circle the phrase "in Christ" or "in Him" every time it appears. Find at least seven ways we are blessed in Christ.

REFLECT In Christ, God has "blessed us by giving us every spiritual blessing in the heavenly world" (v. 3 TEV). Some days we may not feel blessed. Some days we may not show the changed lives we possess in Christ. On those days—and every day—consciously focusing on *where* we are can help us remember *who* we are.

Repeat after me: We are in Christ. That means we are:

1. CHOSEN (v. 4). Before God made the world, He chose us. Knowing we would believe in Christ Jesus, the Father picked us out to be His own.

40

2. HOLY (v. 4). No, not snooty about our "goodness." Instead, set apart to Jesus, as a bride is set apart to her husband.

3. BLAMELESS (v. 4). No, not sinless. Made pure by the cleansing blood of Christ.

4. SONS (v. 5). Yes, in God's family, even women are sons. We became God's children when we believed in His only begotten Son. At Jesus' return, we will receive all the privileges of the legally adopted male heir who has just come of age.

5. "ACCEPTED IN THE BELOVED" (v. 6 KJV). God the Father has chased us down to give us all the good gifts that are ours in Jesus.

6. REDEEMED (v. 7). Thanks to Jesus, we who were enslaved by sin have been set free. The awesome price paid to free us? Christ's own lifeblood.

7. FORGIVEN (v. 7). Because Jesus took the punishment for our offenses, God has dropped all charges against us.

8. WISE (v. 8). The Father has given us insight into His eternal plan, purposes, and principles.

9. UNDERSTANDING (v. 8). The Father has provided us the practical ability to discern His will.

10. ABLE TO KNOW HIS SECRET PLANS (v. 9). God has made known to us truths no human knew until Christ's death and resurrection, truths such as His plan "to bring all creation together, everything in heaven and on earth, with Christ as head" (v. 10).

11. GOD'S HEIRS—AND HIS HERITAGE (v. 11). We are due to inherit all God owns; our Lord has inherited us. Think of it. Not only do we have access to unimaginable riches in Christ, but also the God who made the universe counts Himself rich in us.

12. SEALED (v. 13). The moment we believed in Jesus, the Holy Spirit came to live inside us. He became God's "stamp of ownership" (v. 13) on us, showing us that we are God's and we are secure.

13. GUARANTEED (v. 14). The indwelling Spirit also became to us God's guarantee of more to come. He is God's pledge that we who belong to Him will one day inherit all that is His.

We are blessed women! But we don't dare get haughty

about it. We know there is no room for pride in Christ—because anyone can enter, and no one deserves to be able to do so.

How, then, do we respond when we realize who we are in Christ? What do we do when we grasp the awesome changes our new position has made in our lives?

Praise (v. 3)! Praise (v. 6)! Praise (v. 12)! Praise (v. 14)!

Look again at Ephesians 1:3. The first word of that verse in Greek is a form of the verb *eulogetos*, to bless. It literally means "to speak well of."

Read the similar refrains in verses 6, 12, and 14. All contain the word *epainos*. It denotes intense praise, commendation.

We praise God—not only when we feel good, and not merely by feeling good about Him. Praise doesn't rely on feelings. Praise is an act of the will.

We bless God when we choose to tell good things about Him to Him or to others. We bless Him when we act in ways that give Him glory. We praise our Lord when we openly, wholeheartedly speak out the truth of who He is and what He's done.

Knowing we are in Christ, "let us praise God for his glorious grace" (v. 6 TEV). With our lips, with our lives, let's speak well of Him.

REPROGRAM   Memorize 1 Timothy 4:12.

RESPOND   Offer a personal praise prayer to God based on Ephesians 1:3-14. Notice today: Do your words and actions speak well of your God?

DAY 15

We're Southern Baptist women

You don't have to be Southern Baptist to be saved. On the other hand, you don't need to mumble when someone asks your denomination.

Nehemiah might have been tempted to mumble when asked his nationality. His people, the Jews, had been taken captive into Babylon. Years later, a remnant had returned to Judah; but they were "in great difficulty." They served a Persian monarch. "The foreigners who lived nearby looked down on them" (Neh. 1:3 TEV). The wall of their capital city, Jerusalem, lay in ruins.

Though cupbearer to the Persian king Artaxerxes, Nehemiah gladly identified with his suffering people. He believed them to be a God-called people with a God-appointed task. Having obtained the king's consent, he went to Jerusalem with a plan.

READ Nehemiah 2:17-18; 4:6; 6:15-16; Romans 15:4-7. Give three reasons Nehemiah's rebuilding project was a success.

REFLECT Under Nehemiah's leadership, the Jews rebuilt the Jerusalem wall in record time. Their triumph did not mean they encountered no obstacles. Indeed, they faced constant opposition from without, as well as squabbles within. What, then, were the secrets of their success?

1. THEY BUILT ON A SURE FOUNDATION. Before deciding to start the work, Nehemiah surveyed the parts of the old wall that remained (Neh. 2:13-15). Even more

important, he made sure an invisible foundation for rebuilding had been laid. It consisted of two raw materials: the Word of God and prayer.

God's Word declared, "Your people will rebuild what has long been in ruins, building again on the old foundations. You will be known as the people who rebuilt the walls" (Isa. 58:12 TEV).

Nehemiah discovered his part in God's plan through fasting and prayer. He prayed until God told him what to do. He kept praying until God opened a way for him to do it (Neh. 1:1-2:6). He prayed while the building was in progress (4:4-5; 6:14) and even after the work was done (13:14,29,31).

2. THE PEOPLE WORKED TOGETHER. When Nehemiah challenged the Jews to rebuild, they were unanimous in their response: "Let's start rebuilding!" (2:18 TEV). Immediately, they backed up their words with actions. "They got ready to start the work" (2:18 TEV).

Priests, villagers, goldsmiths, perfumers, city officials, Levites, and merchants worked shoulder to shoulder (Neh. 3). All labored together, not because they were forced to do so, but because they "were eager to work" (4:6 TEV). The task had become personally important to each one.

3. THEY DEALT WITH EACH PROBLEM AS IT AROSE. When the builders received word that their enemies were planning to attack, they prayed and set up a guard "day and night" (4:9). The work continued, but each builder carried a weapon. Designated servants were responsible solely to hold extra armor.

When some of the Jews began treating others unfairly, Nehemiah called the wrongdoers to account. He urged them to give up their wrong practices. To their credit, the people replied, "We'll do as you say" (5:12 TEV).

4. THEY RELIED ON GOD. Before beginning the work, Nehemiah told Israel's enemies, "The God of Heaven will give us success" (2:20 TEV). When facing attack, Nehemiah declared, "Our God will fight for us" (4:20 TEV). The wall was completed in only 52 days. At that point, the Jews' enemies "knew that the work had been done with God's help" (6:16 TEV).

The Jews' God-given task was not finished with the

completion of Jerusalem's wall. Their great task was to give to the world the Messiah. In order to survive to accomplish that task, though, the remnant first had to build a protecting wall.

Southern Baptists, too, are a God-called people with a God-appointed task. Our task? To give worldwide witness that the Messiah has come. Like the Jews, we face great opposition from without, great struggles within. In order to survive to complete our mission, we too must build a wall—not of isolation, but of protection.

How? We must continue to build all we do on the firm foundation of the Word of God and prayer. We must seek to "be of the same mind with one another according to Christ Jesus" (Rom. 15:5 NASB). We must employ God's wisdom to handle problems as they arise. We must rely solely on our God to give us success.

Before the Jewish exile, God "looked for someone who could build a wall, who could stand in the places where the walls have crumbled and defend the land . . . but, I could find no one" (Ezek. 22:30 TEV). In Nehemiah's day, God found a man—and then a people—to build a wall.

May we, as Southern Baptist women, be modern-day rebuilders of broken walls.

REPROGRAM   Repeat 1 Timothy 4:12. Review 1 Peter 2:9-10.

RESPOND   List positive things about Southern Baptists for which you are grateful. Thank God for each thing you listed. Be a wall builder: pray Romans 15:5-6 for our denomination and its leaders.

WHO ARE WE?

We're young women

The pilot taxis his aircraft onto the runway. He presses the throttle forward until the entire plane vibrates with the power of the engine. That power, rightly harnessed and directed, can lift plane and passengers into the air. Unharnessed or misdirected, the same power can prove fatal.

Youth has its own awesome power. We as young women have energies and emotions that can destroy, if not properly channeled. To find out how one person kept the power of her young womanhood under God's strong hand, let's take a look at Esther.

READ   Esther 2:8-20. List characteristics of Esther you would like to develop.

REFLECT   Growing up, Esther probably did not aspire to be queen of Persia. She was a Jew in exile and an orphan. A virgin, she likely expected to marry a young Jewish man chosen for her by her uncle and guardian Mordecai.

But one day the king's overseer appeared at her door. "Come with me," he told her. She went, and found herself living in the king's palace, along with many other beautiful, young virgins. She had been drafted into what we today would consider a most degrading beauty pageant. After a year of preparation, each of the "contestants" had to spend a night with the king. One young lady would "win." She would be crowned queen. The others could not take their hurt pride and go home to marry and rear families. For the rest of their lives, they would live as women the king had slept with and rejected. They would carry the title *concubine*.

Faced with the prospect of such a future, Esther could easily have become bitter or rebellious. I've kept myself pure for this? she might have thought. But if she felt bitterness, she conquered it.

Esther maintained such a sweet attitude that she quickly won the favor of Hegai, the eunuch in charge of the harem. He gave her the best place in the harem and treated her better than any of the other women (v. 9).

Esther could have grown condescending toward others. But if she felt pride, she did not let it have its way. Rather, she deferred to sound advice given by Hegai and Mordecai (vv. 10, 15).

In preparing for her night with the king, Esther could have become intimidated. She could have looked at all the other beautiful women around her and thought, "I'll never be the one. It's hopeless." Or, she could have racked her brain to come up with a gimmick, something that would have made her stand out from all the others. Instead, taking any fears she had in hand, she chose simply to be herself. She went in to the king taking only what Hegai had recommended.

Through the whole experience, Esther did what the apostle Paul would later instruct Timothy to do: "Do not let anyone look down on you because you are young, but be an example for the believers in your speech, your conduct, your love, faith, and purity" (1 Tim. 4:12 TEV).

Most of us do not have the beauty Esther possessed. None of us faces the same circumstances she faced. But all of us do have energies and emotions, just as she did. When we give those energies free reign, they can hurt and destroy. When we commit them into the strong hand of our God, He will channel them effectively.

We can run roughshod over others in our zeal to accomplish a mission, for example; or we can, by God's grace, exercise restraint and courtesy. We can nurse hurt feelings when our efforts go unnoticed, or we can leave our hurt at the feet of Jesus and keep on doing what needs to be done.

We can live at the mercy of our desires; or we can deny ourselves, put our desires in Christ's hands, and watch as He changes them. We can turn our energies to frivolous things, thinking ourselves too young for important tasks, or we can accept whatever challenges God lays before us.

A young man, Jeremiah, protested when God called him to be a prophet to the nations (Jer. 1:4). God responded to Jeremiah, "Do not say that you are too young, but go to the people I send you to, and tell them everything I command you to say" (Jer. 1:7 TEV).

That one young man did indeed proclaim God's truth to nations. His words still resound today.

One young woman, Esther, became a queen, saved her nation, and, in the process, managed to grow even more beautiful on the inside. Her example still shines today. Like Esther, let us make the most of our days as young women. Whatever our energies and emotions, let us keep them under the firm hand of our God.

REPROGRAM Repeat from memory 1 Timothy 4:12; 1 Peter 2:9-10; 2 Timothy 2:21.

RESPOND When you think of the older WMU members of your church, are you intimidated? secretly condescending? Ask God to keep you from either wrong attitude and to develop in you an attitude of loving appreciation.

D A Y   1 7

WHO ARE WE?

We're missioning women

Think of three things that *take in* but don't *give out*. Got your list in mind? OK. Here's mine:
1. The Dead Sea
2. A clogged fountain
3. A potbellied, armchair athlete

None of the above makes a very pretty picture. Is that true of the items on your list?

Taking in is vital to life. We would not live long without eating or drinking, for example. But taking in is only half the cycle. It's drawing a breath and holding it. It's eating but never exercising. Taking in is completed by giving out.

READ   Matthew 9:35-10:8. Using this passage as a springboard, list things the disciples received from Jesus.

REFLECT   Jesus invested a lot in His disciples. He put much prayer into their calling (see Luke 6:12-13). He put much time and energy into their training.

In the cities and villages of Galilee, He gave them firsthand experience of His power to preach, teach, and heal. He gave them insight into His deep love for people. At the proper time, He gave them both authority and instructions.

The disciples were hungry to receive from Jesus. They took in as much as they could of what He gave out. Although their understanding was limited, they somehow knew that what He offered could change lives.

Just before His crucifixion, Jesus thanked the Father for His followers' receptivity. He prayed, "I gave them

49

the message that you gave me, and they received it" (John 17:8 TEV).

Yet Jesus knew that, in order to be spiritually fit, His disciples must give as well as receive. Soon after calling the 12, He started them on an exercise program we might call "missioning."

It began with a warm-up stretch. You see, Jesus had seen the distress of the multitudes. He had hurt for them (Matt. 9:36). But the disciples' eyes and hearts had apparently grown stiff with disuse. To limber up His followers spiritually, Jesus prescribed prayer: "Pray to the owner of the harvest that he will send out workers to gather in his harvest" (Matt. 9:38 TEV).

The Lord knew that, as the disciples prayed, they too would begin to see the fields of souls ready for harvesting. They would begin to desire to gather these souls. They would be warmed up, ready to go, when the summons for service came.

And the summons did come. To those who had been praying, Jesus said, "Go" (10:7).

Of course, He first provided them with the necessary equipment. He gave them His authority and complete instructions. But having the paraphernalia would have done them no good if they hadn't put it to use. New jogging suits hanging in a closet never took a pound off anyone.

The disciples went out to minister and witness. They had heard Jesus' powerful words. They had seen His powerful deeds. Now Jesus told them, "Freely you received, freely give" (Matt. 10:8 NASB).

We, too, have received freely from Jesus. We have received His holy Word. We have taken spiritual and material blessings He has poured out on us. We have accepted prayers, encouragement, and kind deeds from those acting in His name. We have gained knowledge of missions needs and missionaries' doings worldwide.

We too will stay spiritually fit only by giving as freely as we have received. If we fail to pray, we will soon find our hearts unmoved and our bodies unmoving when God reveals a need. If we fail to minister and witness, we will grow fat and complacent.

As missioning women, we *want* to give freely. So, as

God directs, we take action. We give extra, focused prayertime to missions needs. We teach other women and children about the mission God has entrusted to us. We give sacrificially to missions causes. We find ways to care for missionaries and their families. We spend vacation time doing volunteer missions work. We reach out to the needy with practical helps given in Jesus' name. We speak out the good news that Jesus saves.

Of course, we don't *all* do everything. But, as missioning women, we each do something. We listen for Jesus' instructions, and when the summons comes, we are ready.

We don't consider our mission "accomplished" just because we have taken action once. We know that, for exercise to do any good, it must be repeated consistently. And so, we keep missioning.

REPROGRAM Memorize Romans 12:3.

RESPOND If you haven't before, begin now thinking of yourself as a missioning woman. Make two lists: (1) How I Am Taking in the Lord's Words and Ways; (2) How I Am Giving out What I've Received. What one thing can you do to make your lists more balanced?

WHO ARE WE?

We're unique women— unique as persons

Fannie wrote powerfully, spoke eloquently, and led confidently. A single woman, she was known for her grace and poise.

Ethlene built her life on faith, prayer, and study. A beautiful woman, she had great personal magnetism and public-speaking skill. Yet she handled behind-the-scenes service and tedious details well.

Marie had amazing ability to organize, motivate, and promote. Enthusiastic, smiling, she loved both interior decorating and pageantry.

Dorothy earned three doctorates while carrying on three careers and rearing three children. Amazingly, she is in delicate health.

Fannie Heck, Ethlene Cox, Marie Mathis, Dorothy Sample—all unique women—have all served as president of Woman's Missionary Union, SBC.

READ Genesis 49:1-28. Mark adjectives and word pictures Jacob used to describe his sons. (Example: Reuben—proud, strong, like a raging flood.)

REFLECT God never mass produces. He gave Jacob 12 sons—each of them different. To date, He has given Woman's Missionary Union 14 presidents—each unique.

On his deathbed, Jacob assembled his sons to tell them what would happen to them in the future. After recording Jacob's words, the inspired writer of Genesis said, "He blessed them, every one with the blessing appropriate to him" (Gen. 49:28 NASB).

Jacob recognized his sons' differences. He built his statement of what each would do on his knowledge of the qualities each possessed. Judah, for example, had shown strong leadership ability. Jacob called him a *lion* (v. 9).

Jacob termed Issachar a *donkey* (v. 14), knowing that his son would rather serve than fight. Dan, Jacob pictured as a *serpent* (v. 17); Naphtali, as a *doe* (v. 21); Joseph, as a *vine* (v. 22); Benjamin, as a *wolf* (v. 27).

Jacob's words to his sons were blessings, not flatterings. As a wise father, he told his sons the truth, even when the truth contained reprimand or reproach.

Ordinarily, the firstborn received his father's birthright. Yet, Jacob passed the birthright to fourth-born Judah. Why?

Jacob saw severe character flaws in his three oldest sons. Those flaws had led each of the three to commit great sins that remained unconfessed. Reuben, uncontrolled as "a raging flood" (v. 4), had gone to bed with his father's concubine. Simeon and Levi had "killed men in anger" (v. 6).

By exposing his sons' flaws, Jacob gave them opportunity to face their weaknesses and turn them into strengths. Levi's descendants, to their credit, did just that (see Ex. 32:25-29).

Like Jacob's sons, we Baptist Young Women have one heavenly Father. Thus, we are all family members—yet we are all unique. We can capitalize on our uniquenesses if we will learn from Jacob some practical tips for blessing one another.

First, Jacob blessed his sons, not by thinking good thoughts about them, but by speaking good words to them. If we would give a blessing, we too must speak out. We must say the good things we think.

Second, Jacob spoke words appropriate to each son. He did not lump all 12 together or try to make any of them what they were not. His blessings celebrated their individuality.

If we would bless, we, like Jacob, must receive others as they are. Instead of trying to make everyone the same, let us delight in our differences. In so doing, we free one another to fulfill the respective purposes for which God has created us.

For the most part, Jacob spoke encouraging words. He pointed his sons toward the future with hope. As a father, he also spoke rebuking words when needed. But even then, he spoke the truth in love.

Many of us say far too few encouraging words. In order to bless, we must "not use harmful words, but only helpful words, the kind that build up and provide what is needed" (Eph. 4:29 TEV).

If rebuke is necessary, let us make certain we are speaking from the right position (personal purity and close friendship) and with the right attitude (desire to restore). Let us speak always "in a spirit of gentleness" (Gal. 6:1 NASB).

Above all, Jacob's words echoed his commitment to his sons. He had spent years rearing them. Now that he was approaching death, he continued to care what happened to them. His blessings gave him a stake in their future.

Let us live lives that show our commitment to one another. Then, when we say appropriate, encouraging words, our words will have the power to bless.

REPROGRAM Practice saying Romans 12:3 from memory. Review 1 Timothy 4:12.

RESPOND Jot down the names of those in your BYW organization. Beside each name, write unique aspects of that person's background, personality, etc. Think of a word picture you might use to describe each woman. Plan to bless at least one young woman on your list by complimenting her for some aspect of her life that you admire.

WHO ARE WE?

We are unique women— unique in giftedness

To learn the size of your head, would you lay it down on a foot measure? To discover the size of your foot, would you try to fit it into a hat?

Absurd questions. But we are sometimes just as absurd in our attempts to measure faith—faith of ourselves and others. We tend to use the "comparison method": We mentally compare our doings to others' doings and thus try to gauge which of us has faith and how much. That works about as well as comparing a head to a foot.

In Romans 12, Paul urged believers to use a much more reliable measure of faith—the "spiritual gift method."

READ   Romans 12:3-8. Underline the spiritual gifts named in these verses. How does each gift relate to faith (see vv. 3, 6)?

REFLECT   What was Paul urging when he wrote, "Think of yourself . . . in accordance with the measure of faith God has given you" (Rom. 12:3 NIV)?

The Greek word translated *measure* can mean "that which is measured." In that case, Paul was saying, "Judge yourself according to the amount of faith that God has given you" (TEV).

The word *measure* can also mean "that which is used for measuring." Thus understood, the verse indicates that God has given each believer a faith-measuring gauge. The gauge? Spiritual giftedness.

All Christians are gifted (see 1 Cor. 12:7). All have

special abilities that God bestowed at conversion and that He energizes as needed. Yet, all Christians do not see their gifts operating fully.

Why? The gifts are an outpouring of God's grace (Rom. 12:6). In salvation, God's grace must be received by faith. In giftedness, God's grace must be employed by faith. The more vigorously we exercise our faith in God, the more effectively we will use our spiritual gifts to serve others.

If we are truly born again yet see little or no evidence of giftedness in our lives, we can know that our faith level is low. Either we have not been stepping out in faith, or we have been placing our faith in the wrong things.

Perhaps we have taken the comfortable route. We have sat back and let others in our BYW organization do the work. We have not visited the nursing home or led a mission study or given sacrificially—because of fear. We have tried to walk by sight, not by faith.

Or perhaps we have taken the self-reliant route. We have had as our attitude, "I can do all things," but we have failed to add, "through Him who strengthens me" (Phil. 4:13 NASB). We have put forth great human effort; we have exercised our natural abilities; but still we have shown no supernatural giftedness. We have seen no supernatural results.

Once we begin to exercise faith in God and His Word, we will surprise ourselves. We will find ourselves doing things we may be naturally hesitant to do—and we will delight in the doing. We will find we have gone beyond the natural realm into the supernatural.

We will discover our special abilities to prophecy (speak God's truth) or teach (explain God's truth) or show mercy or serve or _____ (you fill in the blank). And a wonderful upward spiral will begin.

The more we use our gifts, the greater our faith will grow. The greater our faith grows, the more opportunity we will have to use our gifts.

We will have new power to do new things—but we won't all do the same things. Paul said, "We have different gifts" (Rom. 12:6 NIV). The God who gave those gifts daily provides each believer different directions for using her gifts.

One may cry with a bereaved family, while another prepares a meal for the family. One may teach a woman to read, while another gives the same woman some good used clothes. One may send encouraging notes to an MK (missionary kid), while another invites the MK into her home.

A BYW member cannot measure her faith by others' actions. She can only measure her faith by the extent to which she is obeying God and seeing her spiritual gifts operating. If she is doing what God has told her to do in the power God gives, she is doing well.

The fact that each of us is strong where others are weak makes us mutually dependent. Paul said, "We are all joined to each other as different parts of one body" (Rom. 12:5 TEV).

In a body, we cannot successfully compare the head to the feet, but we can use the feet to get the head where it wants to go, and we can use the head to show the feet the path.

Let's learn a lesson from the body. When it comes to gifts, let's not compare, but share.

REPROGRAM   Repeat from memory Romans 12:3; 1 Timothy 4:12; and 1 Peter 2:9-10.

RESPOND   Look over your list of BYW members. Have you been comparing yourself with anyone on that list? If so, ask God's forgiveness. Thank Him that He has gifted each BYW member in a different way. Thank Him for the spiritual abilities He gave you at salvation. Ask Him to strengthen your faith so that you may use your gifts more effectively.

D A Y 2 0

WHO ARE WE?

We are unique women— unique in ministries

When you hear the word *ministries*, what comes to mind? The duties of pastors, missionaries, and other full-time Christian workers?

In the Bible, *ministry* simply means *service*. A Christian ministers any time she does something in Jesus' name to benefit someone else.

READ 1 Corinthians 12:4-11; John 12:1-3. How were Mary's and Martha's ministries unique? How did the sisters' ministries blend?

REFLECT When an ensemble sings in harmony, each voice sings a unique part, yet each part blends with the others. When the church functions in harmony, each believer performs a unique ministry, yet each ministry blends with the others.

Early in Jesus' ministry, Mary sat at His feet. Her sister Martha, fuming, set the table. At the end of Jesus' ministry, we find Martha still serving tables and Mary still at Jesus' feet.

The two sisters never sang the same note, when it came to ministry. Yet they learned to harmonize. Both offered pleasing service to their Lord when each ministered out of her own gifts and abilities.

Yes, "There are different ways of serving, but the same Lord is served" (1 Cor. 12:5 TEV).

To help improve the blend of ministries in your BYW organization, ask yourself these questions:

1. AM I SINGING? Do I remain silent when God is

prompting me to volunteer? Do I rely on others to tackle jobs I would really like to do, just because they have always done those things?

In our church choir, we have some "whisperers." They hold up their music and open their mouths—but very little sound comes out. The absence of a few voices may not be noticed much in a large choir; but in a group where each person sings a different part, even one person's silence detracts from the sound.

God never doubles up parts. He gives to each believer a unique ministry. If you do not sing your part, it will go unsung.

2. AM I SINGING TOO LOUDLY? Do I hog the show? Do I put so much emphasis on *my* mission action project or *my* enlistment ideas or *my* achievement goals that nobody else's ideas can be heard?

Many choirs have a singer whose voice is heard above the rest. Her singing doesn't impress people, but irritates them. It robs them of the power and beauty of the music.

If you think you have been overbearing in any area, back off and listen. You will create a much better blend when you can hear clearly what those around you are saying and doing.

3. AM I SINGING THE CORRECT PART? Am I trying to do tasks unsuited to my personality and gifts, simply because others expect it of me or I expect it of myself? Have my interests changed—but my tasks stayed the same? Do I take joy in serving, or do I constantly have to make myself do the work required?

When I was in children's choir, my minister of music wanted me to sing alto. I had a high, first-soprano voice. Because he asked, I sang alto—but I didn't enjoy it, nor did I sing it very well. Now that I am an adult, my voice sounds best in a medium range. I sing second soprano. It fits me.

Any job has its tedious parts. But if a job within the church is a constant drudgery to you, it is probably the wrong job for you. When it comes to ministry, let's learn to say no when God says no and yes when He says yes.

4. AM I TRYING TO SING TOO MANY PARTS? Am I carrying all the load, or most of it, myself? Am I always

tired from having too much responsibility? Do I have so many things to do that I cannot do any of them well? Have I accepted tasks because of my concern that they get done rather than because of my assurance that God has called *me* to do them?

It is physically impossible for a person to sing more than one vocal part at one time. That should tell us something. Yet, many of us who love the Lord try to do too many ministries.

When we accept tasks God has not called us to do, we are courting discouragement. We are asking for burnout. In addition, we are standing in the way of the ones He *has* called. We are not giving the Lord room to deal with those persons until they respond.

If you are overloaded, claim the promise of Matthew 7:7. Ask, seek, knock—until God raises up others to share the burdens of responsibility.

In seeking fellow workers, be sensitive to others' gifts and callings. Approach those God lays on your heart gently, realizing that some who are not involved in ministry may have given up in the past after trying to sing the wrong part or too many parts.

Musical blend takes work. It requires listening and wise singing. Harmony of ministry also takes work. But it is worth the effort, for it glorifies God. Let's serve Him together, differently.

REPROGRAM Repeat all six previously learned memory verses: Ephesians 2:10; 2 Timothy 2:21; Colossians 3:12; 1 Peter 2:9-10; 1 Timothy 4:12; Romans 12:3.

RESPOND Ask God to teach you to blend in ministry with other Baptist Young Women.

D A Y 2 1

WHAT ARE WE GOING TO DO?

We're going to obey God

In 1888, God impressed on Annie Armstrong the command to "go forward." She obeyed, and Woman's Missionary Union was born.

WMU is alive and well today because our leaders through the years have committed themselves to obeying God. Individual WMU organizations have risen and remained strong, or faltered and died, because of obedience—or the lack of it.

We, today, have a choice. We can follow Annie Armstrong's example, or we can follow King Saul's.

READ 1 Samuel 15:1-23. Find phrases that show the difference between what God commanded and what Saul did. Find phrases that show the difference between what Saul did and what he said happened.

REFLECT King Saul never learned the lesson of obedience. Prior to the episode recorded in 1 Samuel 15, Saul had disobeyed God in another battle situation.

He had faced a Philistine army of "thirty thousand war chariots, six thousand horsemen, and as many soldiers as there are grains of sand on the seashore" (1 Sam. 13:5 TEV). The Philistines had already "launched a strong attack" (13:6 TEV) on Israel. Yet, the prophet Samuel had told Saul to wait seven days at Gilgal with his gathered army until Samuel came to offer sacrifices and to tell Saul what to do (10:8).

On the seventh day, the king panicked. He began offering the sacrifices himself. Catching Saul in the act, Samuel cried out, "What have you done?" (1 Sam. 13:11 TEV).

Later, when God sent Saul into battle against the Amalekites, He again gave Israel's king specific instructions: "Go and attack the Amalekites and completely destroy everything they have. Don't leave a thing" (1 Sam. 15:3 TEV).

Once again, Saul tried to revise God's agenda. He picked which instructions he would obey and which he would ignore. Did he, then, spare the women and children, out of compassion? No. He spared the Amalekite king and the best animals, out of greed (1 Sam. 15:9). Yet, Saul had the audacity to tell Samuel, "I have obeyed the Lord's command" (1 Sam. 15:13 TEV). When Samuel confronted the king with evidence of his disobedience, Saul had his excuses ready:

• "My men . . . kept the best sheep and cattle" (v. 15 TEV). (He tried to shift the blame.)
• "To offer as a sacrifice to the Lord your God" (v. 15 TEV). (He tried to hide his motives.)

Saul counted partial obedience as obedience; God counted it rebellion. Saul insisted, "I did obey the Lord. . . . But" (vv. 20, 21). God's spokesman said, "You rejected the Lord's command" (v. 23).

Samuel pronounced Saul's sin as heinous as witchcraft. As a result of it, God rejected Saul from being king.

We can learn some things from Saul. We can learn not to try to revise God's marching orders. If the Lord's chosen king could not get away with partial obedience, neither can we. "For he who does wrong will receive the consequences of the wrong which he has done, and that without partiality" (Col. 3:25 NASB).

We can learn to 'fess up. If God's chosen king could not rationalize his sin, neither can we.

We can learn to keep our love for God strong. The first time Saul disobeyed God in a battle situation, Samuel put his finger on the cause: Saul was not a man "after [God's] own heart" (see 1 Sam. 13:13-14). He did not love the Lord above all else.

Jesus said, "If you love Me, you will keep My commandments" (John 14:15 NASB). That's not an attempt at coercion; it's a statement of fact.

To that statement, He added this promise: "And I will

ask the Father, and He will give you another Helper, that He may be with you forever; that is the Spirit of truth, whom the world cannot receive, because it does not behold Him or know Him, but you know Him because He abides with you, and will be in you" (John 14:16-17 NASB).

Baptist Young Women, we don't have to follow in Saul's footsteps. We have received Jesus Christ as Lord. We love Him. We have His Holy Spirit, the Enabler, within. As a result, we have power to live a life of obedience.

Therefore, let's make up our minds even before we face a specific decision that when decision time comes, we will obey God. Let's beware of obeying the Lord partly—and trying to convince ourselves that that is enough. Let's avoid the dire consequences of disobedience. Let's do what God says.

REPROGRAM Memorize 1 Samuel 15:22.

RESPOND Ask God to show you any area of your life in which you have only partially obeyed Him. Ask Him to show you any area in which your BYW organization has not obeyed fully. Commit yourself to do exactly what God says.

D A Y   2 2

WHAT ARE WE GOING TO DO?

We're going to use our God-given resources

How do you respond when you face:
• a hard time in your life?
• a difficult task?
• someone in crisis?
• the daily grind one day too many?

In these or other situations, do you sometimes feel you have gone to the well—and found it dry? Or have you learned to draw from the deep reservoir of resources God has given each of us?

Remember Moses' mother? If ever a woman used her resources wisely, she did.

READ Exodus 1:22-2:10. Make a list of the resources you believe Jochebed drew upon.

REFLECT Jochebed wanted to save her baby. But she was a Hebrew slave in Egypt. Her resources seemed nonexistent. Undaunted, Jochebed took stock of the little she did have.

She had time. She had a basket, tar, and pitch. She had a boy baby and an older daughter. She had creativity, courage, stamina, and faith in God.

Where had she gotten those resources? From God. In 1 Chronicles 29:14, King David acknowledged, "Everything is a gift from you [Lord]" (TEV). Jochebed could have echoed that statement.

What, then, did she do with the resources God entrusted to her? She used her time to nurse Moses through the fragile first three months of life. Then, with her basket, tar, pitch, and creativity, she made him a watertight boat. Using courage, she left her son in the boat at the river's edge. She summoned stamina to help her stay away.

At that point, her two little "human resources" came into play. The baby himself cried real tears, tears that touched an Egyptian princess' heart. The daughter, Miriam, ran up at just the right moment—after the princess had seen the crying child and before she had time to think, "What would *I* do with a baby?" With one well-worded question, Miriam influenced the princess to save Moses' life.

Jochebed's faith in God undergirded all her other resources. Hebrews 11:23 says, "It was faith that made the parents of Moses hide him for three months after he was born" (TEV).

When Jochebed, by faith, tapped into her God-given resources, God moved in to deliver her child.

As individuals and as BYW organizations, we, too, have problems. Daily we face trials, frustrations, and crises. Yet whatever the challenges, our Lord has provided us the resources to meet them.

If we would use those resources wisely, we must first know that God is the owner. We are the stewards, or managers, of what our sovereign Lord has entrusted to us.

We must then see the vastness and variety of the resources we've been given. Like Jochebed, we have time. We have money and possessions. We have family and friends from whose wisdom or abilities we can draw. We have spiritual qualities and gifts, positive character traits, and talents. We have the promises of God's Word, including Philippians 4:19: "And with all his abundant wealth through Christ Jesus, my God will supply all your needs" (TEV).

Finally, we must realize that God requires of stewards one thing—faithfulness (1 Cor. 4:2).

A faithful steward doesn't hoard the resources God has given her. She tithes—and gives beyond the tithe—to God's purposes, particularly missions. She opens her home to those who cannot repay her hospitality. She volunteers time and talents to help others in Jesus' name. She gives the casserole, the ten dollars, the note of appreciation, or the listening ear to a friend, family member, or stranger, as God directs.

A faithful steward doesn't leave her resources untapped. Whether Jesus has entrusted her with many talents or one, she thanks Him and wisely invests what she has. If she can hold babies and sing to them about Jesus, she does it—without mourning because she can't really sing. If she can cheer the weary, she does—without lamenting because she cannot teach. If she can witness to a neighbor over coffee, she does so—without feeling guilty for not handing out tracts door-to-door.

A faithful steward doesn't squander her resources. She turns off TV programs that make fun of Christian standards and gives her time to more valuable pursuits. She avoids impulse buying and saves her money for God-pleasing expenditures. If she has children, she teaches them early to love God and to love the world He came to save.

Jesus said, "He who is faithful in a very little thing is faithful also in much; and he who is unrighteous in a very little thing is unrighteous also in much" (Luke 16:10 NASB).

Today, let's make a new commitment to use—not abuse—our God-given resources. As we do so, God will move in to work wonders.

REPROGRAM Repeat 1 Samuel 15:22 several times from memory. Review 1 Peter 2:9-10.

RESPOND What needs or difficulties do you face today? What challenges does your BYW organization face? Ask God for wisdom to recognize and use the resources He has given.

WHAT ARE WE GOING TO DO?

We're going to expand our boundaries

Have you ever read aloud (or quoted) John 3:16, inserting your name in place of *the world* and *whosoever?* Do so now. . . .

"For God so loved—me." It's a wonderful place to start the Christian life. It's a good place to come back to from time to time. But it's not the place to set up camp. Too many Christians spend their lives saying, "For God so loved me," but never adding, "and her and him and them. . . ."

The first Christians made a similar mistake. They were Jews, and they tended to believe that Jesus had died to bring salvation to their nation only. God went to great lengths to show them their error.

READ   Acts 11:1-18. Jot down the means God used to confirm to Peter that his world needed enlarging.

REFLECT   I lay in bed reading *Across China* by Peter Jenkins (author of *Walk Across America*).

In 1984, Jenkins, a writer, had gone into Tibet with a team of mountain climbers attempting to scale Mt. Everest. In the Himalayas, Jenkins had experienced some of the effects high altitude causes: extreme nausea, severe headaches, and "Himalayan Hysteria"—a combination of crazy behavior, uncontrollable laughter, and inability to think clearly.

He saw the fierce, isolated conditions under which the Tibetan people live. He felt their gentle yet indomitable spirit and their zest for life.

He learned the religious history of the Tibetans. They had for centuries practiced Buddhism. At one time, the mountain peaks had contained almost 6,000 monasteries. A fourth of the men (about 120,000) had been "holy men." Since Communist takeover in 1951, all but 9 of the monasteries had been destroyed. Fewer than 1,000 holy men remained.

Jenkins was angry that the Communists have so viciously torn from the Tibetan people their centuries-old religion. I was burdened that these simple mountain dwellers have suffered greatly for the lie of Buddhism, are being indoctrinated into the lie of Communism, and have not heard the truth of Christ.

They need to know, too, I thought. But who can get to them to tell them?

I had enjoyed my own cozy world until God opened my eyes to a bigger world—a world that includes the lost men, women, and children of Tibet.

The Apostle Peter enjoyed a cozy world, too. As he saw it, Jesus had died and been resurrected—for the Jews.

Then Peter got stretched. While praying, he saw a vision and heard a message. Both were repeated three times. Afterward, he met three messengers, heard the Holy Spirit's directions, gathered six fellow Christians, and witnessed the outpouring of the Holy Spirit on Cornelius and his household.

That God had to use all those means to enlarge Peter's perspective testifies to the hesitancy of Peter and the Jewish Christians to expand their boundaries. That God *did* use all those means testifies to His determination that His people's boundaries be enlarged.

His perspective widened, Peter gave Cornelius the message of new life in Christ. The Lord hasn't called me to witness in Tibet yet. But He has called me to include that faraway land in my world.

He has also called me to include the people right around me in my world. When my family and I moved to Memphis, Tennessee, our next-door neighbors were black. I had thought that sometime I would go over and introduce myself to them. But I hadn't done it. So God gave me a little shove.

One afternoon, I locked myself and my six-month-old daughter out of the house. Jerry, my husband, was out of town.

I ended up in my neighbor's kitchen, drinking tea with her while waiting for the locksmith to come. Before too many weeks had passed, we had become friends; and I had had several opportunities to talk with her about my faith in the Lord Jesus.

Where do your boundaries need expanding? Do you react to international news with indifference? Do you hesitate to share God's love with persons around you who are different from you in some way?

God has a bigger world for all of us. He wants to take us past the line beyond which we will not step to minister or witness. He wants to take us, in mind and heart, to places and peoples we'll never meet.

It may shake us up, but, after all, "God so loved *the world*, that he gave his only begotten Son, that *whosoever* believeth in him should not perish, but have everlasting life" (John 3:16 KJV, emphases added).

Like Peter, let's step out into God's world.

REPROGRAM   Repeat from memory 1 Samuel 15:22 and Romans 12:3.

RESPOND   Ask God to make you willing to expand boundaries of personal ministry and witness to include anyone to whom He might send you. Ask Him to begin creating world awareness in you by burdening you for one country other than the United States.

D A Y 2 4

WHAT ARE WE GOING TO DO?

We are going to develop our personal quiet times

Are you satisfied with your devotional quiet times? How would you rate them as to:
• Length: Do you meet the Lord daily in Bible study and prayer? Do you give Him as much quality time at each sitting as you believe He desires?
• Breadth: How greatly does your time with God affect the way you act the rest of the day?
• Height: When you read the Bible, is God's presence real to you? When you pray, is God's power unleashed?
• Depth: Does God ever show you deep truths in His Word, jewels you've never mined before?

READ Psalm 119:129-136. Find: (1) terms the psalmist used to describe God's Word, (2) responses the psalmist made to God's Word, and (3) results of knowing and obeying God's Word.

REFLECT Although the writer of Psalm 119 had only a portion of the Bible we have today, he found it contained words for every occasion. It held testimonies of God's works and ways. It gave precepts, commands, and statutes for right living. It included promises for God's people.
The psalmist called God's Word *wonderful* ("far exceeding anything conceived by man," v. 129 Amplified). He longed for God's words. He learned them. He obeyed them. He cried over those who failed to keep them. In short, he counted God's Word very precious. He took it very seriously.

70

If we long for God's words as the psalmist did, we have already taken a giant step toward improved quiet times. The God who gives that desire is willing and able to fulfill it. He says, "Ask, and you will receive; seek, and you will find; knock, and the door will be opened to you" (Matt. 7:7 TEV).

First, *ask*. Pray the words of Psalm 119:133*a*: "Establish my footsteps in Thy word" (NASB). Write those words in the front of your Bible or put them on a card and attach it to your bathroom mirror or your refrigerator. Pray them daily for six weeks.

As you sit down to read the Bible, ask God for understanding and insight. Ask Him to make you aware of His presence. Ask Him to communicate personally with you. As you finish your Bible reading, ask God for grace to live out what you've read.

Second, *seek*. The psalmist said, "In my desire for your commands I pant with open mouth" (v. 131 TEV). One who yearns for something that much will seek it.

Like the psalmist, actively seek a time and place to be alone with God. Don't expect a time just to appear. Satan will make sure one never does.

If a setting doesn't work out, identify the reasons. Then, seek another time or another place. Or seek to remove the hindrances from the setting you've chosen. Keep on seeking until you find.

Be forewarned: When you take a trip, change jobs, get out of school for the summer, get married, have a baby—or any time your life-style changes—your setting for quiet time may vanish. But God is faithful. He will provide a new place and time for you to meet with Him, if only you will seek.

Once you sit down with the Bible, don't just skim its verses. God says, "Look for [My wisdom] as hard as you would for silver or some hidden treasure" (Prov. 2:4 TEV). Seek God's deep truths.

Finally, *knock*. Consider how you would feel if you had accepted a date with a young man and he came to your door—but never knocked. Instead, he stood around for awhile and, when you never opened the door (because you didn't know he was there), he left. Or what if he knocked once; then, without waiting for you to get to the door, he got back in his car and drove away?

What must God think when we treat Him in similar fashion? He hears when we "call" to ask if we can meet with Him regularly. He makes a date to meet us at a certain time and place. He waits for us. But then, the alarm goes off, and we just roll back over. Or the TV show is just too good to turn off. Or we get busy with first one thing and then another until we realize we've missed our allotted time.

If a guy wants a date, he must put his fist to the door and knock. If you want a quiet time, put your body in the chosen setting and "knock": Open your Bible and start reading; open your mouth and start praying. Knock again tomorrow—even if you feel you got no response today.

The psalmist kept opening the Word, regardless of his feelings (see Ps. 119:141, 143). Isaiah once said, "The Lord God helps me . . . Therefore, I have set My face like flint, And I know that I shall not be ashamed" (Isa. 50:7 NASB).

Let's set our faces like flint to have daily quiet times with the living God. Among other things, we'll gain a new perspective on life (v. 130), power over sin (v. 133), victory when ill-treated by others (v. 134), and concern for the lost and backslidden (v. 136). Yes, our God will help us, and we will not be ashamed.

REPROGRAM Memorize Psalm 119:131.

RESPOND Evaluate the strengths and weaknesses of your quiet time. Commit yourself under God to have at least five minutes of Bible reading and five minutes of prayer every day for the next 30 days.

WHAT ARE WE GOING TO DO?

We're going to intercede for the world

Now wait a minute. Do you mean I'm supposed to pray for everything and everyone? I can think of things and people to pray for all day, but I can't possibly intercede for them all. Why, I'm struggling just to have some kind of daily quiet time. And besides, praying for the world is just too big a task. Sometimes, I find myself not interceding at all because I can't pray for it all."

READ 1 Timothy 2:1; Ephesians 6:10-18. What part does prayer play in (1) Paul's first appeal to Timothy, and (2) his final command to the Ephesian church? For whom are we to pray?

REFLECT Interceding for the world is an impossible mission. Yet, it is a mission entrusted to us by God. He commands us to pray for all believers (Eph. 6:18) and to pray for all people (1 Tim. 2:1).

However, it is not one Christian's responsibility to pray for "everything and everyone." God intends that His people intercede for the world together.

What He commands, He enables. As we, through Him, expand our boundaries and develop our quiet times, we will also enlarge the scope of our intercession.

But we must realize this: Intercession will never be easy, for we do not intercede by casually mentioning a name in prayer. True intercession is marching into spiritual battle after having put on God's armor.

Through intercession, we strive to take territory from Satan and his legions. We strive to keep territory from

73

falling into their hands (Eph. 6:12).

Our enemy won't give an inch without a struggle. To keep us from praying, he'll use every trick in his book. He'll appeal to our laziness, apathy, or lack of self-discipline. He'll try to discourage us through changes of schedule, sickness, and hard times. He'll create distractions and interruptions.

Satan doesn't give ground easily, but he must give ground—when God's people intercede: "The prayer of a good person has a powerful effect" (James 5:16 TEV).

So, then, let's "put on all the armor that God gives" (Eph. 6:11 TEV) so we can intercede with power.

1. THE BELT OF TRUTH. The Roman soldier's belt held his garments together and served as a place to hang his armor. Let's know the truth, tell the truth, live the truth. Otherwise, when we enter our prayer closets, we may be going into battle naked.

2. THE BREASTPLATE OF RIGHTEOUSNESS. A soldier's breastplate protected his heart. If we would pray effectively, let us practice right living and so guard our hearts.

3. THE SHOES OF THE GOSPEL OF PEACE. The right shoes gave a soldier sure-footedness. God's good news has provided us two shoes—peace with God and the peace of God. Peace with God happens the instant we become rightly related to Him through faith in Jesus. The peace of God fills us as we trust and obey Him. Before trying to pray for others, let's make sure we're experiencing God's peace.

4. THE SHIELD OF FAITH. The shield protected all the other armor. To keep sin from creeping in and destroying our prayer power, let's trust our God—even when things are darkest, even when it looks as though He has denied Himself.

5. THE HELMET OF SALVATION. The helmet protected the head. To keep doubts from infiltrating our minds and hindering our prayers, let's know that we know we're saved. Let's keep learning all that salvation involves.

6. THE SWORD OF THE SPIRIT. When we speak Scripture in prayer, the enemy must flee. Let's know God's Word so we can wield it with power.

Once we have on the armor, let's get in the battle. How? "Pray on every occasion, as the Spirit leads. . . . Keep alert and never give up" (Eph. 6:18 TEV). To help your praying, you might want to:

Keep a prayer notebook. Write requests and answers in it. Use it during your daily quiet times.

Divide your quiet-time prayer requests among the days of the week. You may, for example, pray for church needs on Sunday, your family on Monday, other believers on Tuesday, personal requests on Wednesday, lost persons on Thursday, your country on Friday, and miscellaneous requests on Saturday. Pray daily for missions needs and for missionaries having birthdays.

Learn to pray "on the spot." When someone asks, "Would you pray for me?" answer, "May I pray with you right now?" Otherwise, you may forget to pray at all.

Turn your thoughts into prayers. When people or needs come to mind, lift them to the Lord. The Holy Spirit may have put that person or event on your heart specifically to prompt you to pray.

Remember: a fervent prayer must be heartfelt, but it doesn't have to be long.

Realize others, too, are interceding. When you go into battle in prayer, you do so as one member of God's vast army.

REPROGRAM Memorize Ephesians 6:18. Review Psalm 119:131.

RESPOND Evaluate the scope and power of your intercessory praying. Set one goal for broadening the scope of your praying. Ask God to make you an international intercessor.

D A Y 2 6

WHAT ARE WE GOING TO DO?

We're going to demonstrate God's love in action

OK, ladies. Time to demonstrate. No, we're not going to carry banners and march. We're going to demonstrate God's love. We're going to show patience and kindness. We're going to act without jealousy, boastfulness, pride, rudeness, or selfishness. We'll not be easily angered. We'll keep no record of wrongs. We'll rejoice when truth prevails. Tirelessly, we'll protect, trust, hope, persevere. We'll show by our actions the love that never fails.

READ Acts 9:32-42. Find at least three persons or groups of persons who showed God's love in action. Identify how each demonstrated God's love.

REFLECT Demonstrations of God's love can take many forms. In Acts 9:32-42, Peter showed God's love through performing miracles. He healed a paralytic; he raised a woman from the dead.

Although most of us haven't received from Jesus that kind of miracle-working power, we can learn from Peter. He showed God's boundless love both to believers and to unbelievers.

Dorcas is identified as a disciple, or believer (v. 36). Aeneas is not. He is called "a certain man" (v. 33 NASB). On finding Aeneas, Peter didn't ask for the man's spiritual credentials. Rather, Peter discovered God's will— and did it.

The Bible does not say that Aeneas became a Christian as a result of being healed. It does not even record whether Aeneas said, "Thank you." Yet Peter did not "take back" what he had done or quit helping those he saw in need. He offered love, regardless—just as his Lord had offered love to him.

Even though Peter did not show God's love in order to get a response, his "mission actions" did reap spiritual results. In Lydda and Sharon, all who saw the healed paralytic "turned to the Lord" (v. 35). In Joppa, many who heard of Dorcas' being raised from the dead "believed in the Lord" (v. 42).

Dorcas demonstrated God's love through simple acts of kindness. God's Word calls her "a certain disciple" (v. 36 NASB). The word translated *certain* is an indefinite pronoun. In other places in the New Testament, the same word is rendered *anyone* or *someone*. Dorcas was not an apostle, a missionary, or a church leader. She was simply a believer, like any one of us.

Yet she didn't sit in a corner and moan, "I'm a nobody." She realized, "I'm someone." And she showed God's love by doing one thing she could: sewing. She didn't just make one garment and then decide, Well, I'm through with that! She "was abounding with deeds of kindness and charity, which she continually did" (v. 36 NASB).

The believers at Joppa demonstrated God's love by seeking help for Dorcas from the right source. They couldn't heal her, but they sought out someone who could. Knowing Dorcas was already dead, the two men sent to get Peter urged him, "Please hurry and come to us" (v. 38 TEV). The widows mourning in Dorcas' room "crowded around [Peter], crying and showing him all the shirts and coats that Dorcas had made while she was alive" (v. 39 TEV). Together, the believers at Joppa showed the kind of love that never gives up.

In our demonstrations of God's love, we can learn from the examples of Peter, Dorcas, and the Joppa Christians. Like Peter, let's offer tangible help to anyone God lays on our hearts. Let's keep offering help in the name of Jesus Christ, regardless of the response we get.

Like Dorcas, let's abound with good deeds. For some of us, that will involve sewing or cooking. For others, it may mean writing encouraging notes, teaching a nonreader, or offering hospitality to internationals.

Working together as Baptist Young Women, we may

help provide for a needy family. We may take turns running errands for an invalid. We may start a Big A Club or an outreach Bible study. We may minister to alcoholics and their families, the homeless, or latchkey children.

Let's not worry about all the things we can't do. Let's simply take the time and make the effort to do the things we can.

Like the disciples at Joppa, let's recognize our limitations. Let's learn that showing God's love means seeking help for others from the right source. Let's identify the persons and agencies in our communities who can give help beyond what we can offer. Then, when appropriate, let's demonstrate God's love by recommending a dentist to a refugee, a Christian counselor to one suffering deep depression, a women's shelter to an abused wife.

We're going to take action because the love of God has been poured out in our hearts (Rom. 5:5). That love seeks an outlet. When it is given without reserve, it multiplies.

REPROGRAM Practice saying from memory Ephesians 6:18, Psalm 119:131, and 1 Samuel 15:22.

RESPOND Ask God to give you a chance to demonstrate His love in action today to (a) a believer, and (b) an unbeliever. Commit yourself to greater involvement in organized BYW mission action.

D A Y 2 7

WHAT ARE WE GOING TO DO?

We're going to give bold witness of Jesus

Are you ready to go?"

"Almost." I was as excited as a kid going to camp. The next day I would travel by plane to Richmond, Virginia, for the WMU Centennial Celebration. For weeks, I'd felt that the Lord was going to use this experience in a mighty way in my life.

"I'm praying for you," my friend Julie told me.

Good, I thought.

"I'm praying you'll have an opportunity to witness to someone along the way—maybe on the plane," she continued.

Oh, dear, I thought.

READ 2 Kings 7:3-9. Why did the lepers do what they did in verse 8? Why did the lepers say what they said in verse 9?

REFLECT The Israelite city of Samaria faced imminent destruction. A Syrian army had besieged the city and cut off its food supply. The siege had lasted so long that some Samaritans had begun resorting to cannibalism (2 Kings 6:24-30).

In desperation, four lepers set out at dusk one day for the Syrian camp. What they found there surprised and overwhelmed them. The Lord had put death to flight. He'd made available to the starving Samaritans new life and vast provision.

Not hesitating, the lepers pounced on the food and wealth they discovered. But soon, they realized: "We

79

shouldn't be doing this! We have good news, and we shouldn't keep it to ourselves. If we wait until morning to tell it, we are sure to be punished" (2 Kings 7:9 TEV). To their credit, they decided to take action: "Let's go right now and tell" (v. 9 TEV).

It was New Year's Day, 1988. I was evaluating the year just past and writing my goals for the one ahead. I haven't talked to an unbeliever about Christ in a long time, I realized.

The Lord's gentle nudge convicted me that I had not done right. Accordingly, I wrote the following among my 1988 goals: To befriend the lost with whom I come in contact by sharing Christ boldly.

Time passed. It was May. Except for one phone call I'd made to an acquaintance, I had witnessed to no one. In spite of my goals and my desire to please the Lord in this area, I still thought, Oh, dear, when Julie told me she was praying I'd have an opportunity to witness during my trip to Richmond.

The Centennial Celebration was wonderful. God did indeed move in my life. The Sunday afterward, I left the motel after the others in my party because I was flying home at a later time.

Traveling to the airport in the car I'd hired, I began talking to the driver, Sunny, a young man who had immigrated to the US from India. He asked, "Why are you here in Richmond?" I told him. He said, "I carried some other WMU ladies to the airport today. You're a lively bunch."

I felt the Holy Spirit's nudge. "That's because we love Jesus, and we know He loves us," I replied.

"And that equals?"

"Joy," I answered.

We talked about what it means to become a Christian, until we reached the airport. Pulling up to the curb, he said, "Oh. We're here already. Let's go back and start this trip all over so we can discuss this some more." How I wished we could have done just that!

The first leg of my flight home was uneventful. After a stopover, I changed seats. A young woman about my age sat down next to me. At first, we both read. But then she struck up a conversation. While we talked, I noticed she had on a cross necklace. Again, I recognized the Spirit's nudge. I said, "I notice you're wearing a cross. Does that mean you're a Christian?"

"I'm trying to be," she replied.

I asked her what she thought a person had to do to become a Christian. "Be good enough," was her reply in a nutshell. Just as I was about to say, "May I tell you what I believe?" she asked, "Would *you* tell *me* how to become a Christian?"

The flight ended without her making a decision to receive Jesus. But I had given bold witness of Christ twice in one day. I felt an exhilaration that had long been missing from my life.

Baptist Young Women, we have good news. We have walked into the vast riches of Christ. These same riches are available to everyone who will receive them. But many around us will die eternally unless we speak out boldly.

We may face rejection by people now if we witness, but we will face the judgment of God one day if we keep silent.

We are His witnesses. We want to tell. We have His Spirit within to empower us to speak the right words at the right time. And once we've spoken, regardless of the response, we'll know the joy of obedience. Let's go right now and tell.

REPROGRAM   Memorize 2 Kings 7:9.

RESPOND   Ask the Lord to give you opportunity and boldness to share your testimony with someone this week. Thank Him ahead of time that He will do it.

DAY 28

WHAT ARE WE GOING TO DO?

We're going to consider active missions involvement

When faced with the nitty-gritty missions question, "Who will go for us?" what do you do?
• Try to look inconspicuous?
• Assume the question is meant for someone else?
• Say, I'll think about that tomorrow?
• Relax, assured that you cannot go?
• Volunteer gladly?
   We may have to conquer obstacles, fears, and doubts when God sounds the call for missions volunteers. But we can't honestly label ourselves *missioning women* until we have answered, "I'm willing, Lord. Do you want to send me?"

   READ   Acts 18:1-3,18-19; Romans 16:1-5. If you have access to a Bible map of Paul's missionary journeys, find Rome, Corinth, and Ephesus. (Cenchreae was a seaport a few miles east of Corinth.)

   REFLECT   Priscilla and her husband, Aquila, were just settling in after a forced move from Rome to Corinth. They were trying to run a family-owned business. Yet, when Paul left Corinth for Ephesus, the couple set sail with him. They served a term as "foreign missionaries" to the Ephesians before going back to Rome to spread the gospel.
   Phoebe was working in the Cenchrean church. She was apparently single. Yet, she journeyed to distant Rome on mission. She may have delivered Paul's letter to the Roman Christians. She also had other tasks to

82

perform. "Give her any help she may need" (Rom. 16:2 TEV), Paul urged the Romans.

Either Priscilla or Phoebe could have said, "I can't accept missions involvement." But both looked beyond circumstances and their feelings, to the will of God.

We too can discover and do God's will regarding active missions involvement. Bob Mumford, in his book, *Take Another Look at Guidance*, offers practical guidelines we can use in our quest.

He compares our finding God's will to a ship's captain finding his way into a safe harbor through a narrow channel. The captain knows he is on course when three carefully placed harbor lights line up. If any of the three lights moves out of line, the ship may wreck.

Mumford suggests that the Christian's three "harbor lights" are God's Word, the Holy Spirit, and circumstances.

1. GOD'S WORD. The Bible breathes missions. Matthew recorded Jesus' final command to His followers: "Go, then, to all peoples everywhere and make them my disciples" (Matt. 28:19 TEV). Luke reminds us that God called two of five church leaders in Antioch to go out as missionaries (Acts 13:1-2).

As we consider active missions involvement, we must first open our Bibles with the question, "Lord, are you calling me?" on our lips. We probably won't find the answer by closing our eyes, flipping the pages, pointing to a verse, and then peeking to see what it says. God's Word will speak to us as we read it systematically, searchingly, with a heart open to know His will.

2. THE HOLY SPIRIT. God's Spirit will never contradict His Word. Rather, the Spirit makes the Word come alive. He enables us to know how what we've read applies to us. He gives us a sense of deep peace when we're headed in the right direction.

As one young woman reads about Priscilla and Aquila, the Spirit may prompt her, "Pray that God will send more couples to the missions fields." Another woman reading the same verses may feel a tugging within to go out as Priscilla did.

The first woman would step out of God's will if, instead of praying, she pursued missions appointment.

The second woman would miss God's will if she chose to stay home and pray.

3. CIRCUMSTANCES. This harbor light can never guide us by itself. Looking only at circumstances, we would all have reasons we cannot go: "I'm married." "I'm single." "I'm in school." "I work." "I have preschool children." "I have aging parents."

God calls women in all these situations into short-term and career missions. He may call you.

If you believe He wants you actively involved in missions, don't try to manipulate your circumstances to make His will happen. Rather, commit your situation into His hands. Trust Him, in His time, to "prepare your way, leveling mountains and hills" (Isa. 45:2 TEV). When He does, you can go confidently, knowing all three harbor lights are lined up.

Who will go for us?

Priscilla and Phoebe did. We're missioning women. We too will go, if He calls.

REPROGRAM Repeat from memory 2 Kings 7:9 and Ephesians 6:18.

RESPOND Tell the Lord you're willing to go out as His missionary. Then ask, "What is Your will for me regarding career missions? Regarding short-term missions?" When the three harbor lights line up, act accordingly.

D A Y   2 9

WHAT ARE WE GOING TO DO?

We're going to help change our world

Israel had grave problems. The Hebrews had entered Canaan about 150 years earlier. They had conquered the land but had failed to drive out all the ungodly peoples. Soon, they began intermarrying with the Canaanites, worshiping idols, and taking part in grossly immoral practices.

As a result of this national sin, Israel sunk into national servitude. The situation seemed hopeless. But one woman wasn't content just to wring her hands in despair. Her name was Deborah.

READ Judges 4:1-7. Jot down several action words you might use to describe Deborah.

REFLECT For 20 years, Jabin terrorized Israel. Deborah must have known that God was using the Canaanite king to judge her people. Yet she didn't go out, rally the crowds, and cry, "Repent!" Rather, she worked quietly behind the scenes to change things. Sitting under a palm tree, she spoke God's truth to those who came seeking it.

Perhaps partly due to her palm-tree prophecies, the Israelites finally cried out for God's help.

The Lord heard their cries. Choosing to intervene once again in His people's behalf, He used Deborah to call Israel to action. He told her that the day had come for sweeping changes. He specified what changes were to be made and how.

Immediately, Deborah spoke out. She sent for Barak,

the military leader God had chosen, told him what God wanted, and challenged him to do it. At his request, she even accompanied him into battle.

When the battle cry sounded, not all Israel responded. No representatives from the tribes of Reuben, Dan, or Asher joined Barak's army. Yet God gave victory. He called out the stars and the Kishon River to fight for His people (Judg. 5:15-21).

After the battle, the Israelites praised the Lord. "And there was peace in the land for forty years" (Judg. 5:31 TEV).

All because one woman dared to call for change.

Our nation has grave problems, too. Abortions take the lives of 1.5 million babies annually. TV sit-coms spit in the face of Christianity, while millions of viewers laugh. Immorality is dressed as sexual activity and hailed as the norm. Homosexuality is touted as an alternate life-style. Alcoholism and drug abuse run rampant among teens and adults. Racial minorities still meet ill treatment. Children's toys and cartoons are laced with violence and occult teachings.

Yet, let's not wring our hands in despair. We serve the God who can still command the stars to fight for us. Like Deborah, we can:

1. LEARN GOD'S MIND. How does the Lord see our nation? What social and moral ills does He want to war against? Let's find out. Let's seek to learn, not only what's wrong, but also what changes God wants to make and how He wants to make them.

2. SPEAK GOD'S TRUTH. Let's inform family, friends, and acquaintances about the issues that burden us. Let's not get mealy-mouthed when it comes to taking a stand.

We may be ridiculed. We may even be harassed. But national repentance will only come as God's truth is proclaimed in every nook of our country.

3. CHALLENGE GOVERNMENT LEADERS. Barak would not have led an Israelite army to fight Sisera if Deborah hadn't challenged him to do so. Our local, state, and national leaders often hover between opinions. We can affect their stances on moral and social issues by encouraging them to make godly choices, and

by praising them when they do. When appropriate, let's write or call our leaders.

4. GET INTO THE BATTLE. As mentioned on Day 25, our first battleground is prayer. Once we know God's mind about an issue, let's petition Him to act. Let's continue to petition until the victory is gained.

As we pray, let's be open to any other actions He prompts us to take.

When Barak's men fought, God routed the enemy. But the fight was not won until the Israelites "pressed harder and harder against [Jabin] until they destroyed him" (Judg. 4:24 TEV).

After the battle, Deborah sang of the soldiers' attitude: "I shall march, march on, with strength" (Judg. 5:21 TEV).

Let us, by God's grace, do what we can to effect social and moral changes in our world. In the midst of the battle, let us march on with strength. In today's dark hours, may we "shine like the rising sun!" (Judg. 5:31 TEV).

REPROGRAM   Say from memory 2 Kings 7:9, Ephesians 6:18, Psalm 119:131, and 1 Samuel 15:22.

RESPOND   What social or moral ill particularly grieves you? If none, pray for God to give you a burden in one area. Otherwise, determine to make the thing that bothers you a matter of regular prayer. Ask God to use you as a change agent in this area.

D A Y   3 0

WHAT ARE WE GOING TO DO?

We're going to do what God has planned

Are you overwhelmed? After contemplating all we Baptist Young Women are going to do, do you feel inadequate? Do you wonder—but are a bit afraid to ask—"What's my part?"

To answer, let's look at the picture of a virtuous woman painted in Proverbs 31. Although the lady portrayed has a husband and children, all women can gain from examining the broad brush strokes of her life. There, we glimpse excellence.

READ Proverbs 31:10-31. Mark or list the good deeds this excellent woman did. List at least five equally good deeds she is not mentioned as having done.

REFLECT We began our devotions by focusing on the picture God paints of us, His children, in Ephesians 2:10: "For we are His workmanship, created in Christ Jesus for good works, which God prepared beforehand, that we should walk in them" (NASB).

According to that verse, what are we in God's eyes? That's right. We're His workmanship, His poem.

What, then, does our Designer intend for us to do? Every good deed possible? No, the "good works, which [He] prepared beforehand" (Eph. 2:10 NASB).

So how do we know what good works He has planned for us? Solomon declared, "To be wise you must first have reverence for the Lord. If you know the Holy One, you have understanding" (Prov. 9:10 TEV).

A woman of excellence, as described in Proverbs 31,

reverences God (Prov. 31:30 TEV). Her reverence spawns insight. Seeing clearly what deeds God desires of her, she does them. The results?

1. A BALANCED LIFE. She provides for the needs of family members and nurtures her relationships with them. She manages the home well. She enjoys challenging work and engages in fulfilling ministry. At the same time, she does not neglect her own physical needs or spiritual growth.

She accomplishes a lot because she focuses her efforts. She "does not eat the bread of idleness" (v. 27 NASB), but neither does she set herself a frantic pace. She maintains a quiet spirit in the midst of an active life.

2. A LIFE OF BLESSING. Her deeds bless others— family members, business associates, those who work for her, and those to whom she ministers. Others, in turn, bless her. "Her children show their appreciation, and her husband praises her" (Prov. 31:28 TEV).

Moreover, the very deeds she has done prove a blessing to her. They become as fruit which she has planted and cultivated and later can eat and enjoy: "Give her of the fruit of her hands; and let her own works praise her in the gates" (v. 31 KJV).

God is making of us excellent women. As we daily reverence Him and seek to know Him better, we too will learn how to limit ourselves to doing the good works He has planned in advance for us to do.

We'll focus our efforts. Some of us will place priority on interceding. Others will concentrate on doing deeds that show God's love. Some will witness often. Some will tackle with vigor their role as change agents. Others will invest much time in volunteer mission service.

We will do what God tells us to do in each of these areas, but we will not try frantically to do all that needs doing in every area. We'll stop expecting more of ourselves than God does.

Our Creator, of course, "knows what we are made of; he remembers that we are dust" (Psalm 103:14 TEV). He won't plan for us to do what He has not equipped us to do. If we will listen and obey, He will guide us into the good works that will please Him and bless others.

Then, knowing we're walking out His plan, we will be able to "smile at the future" (see v. 25 NASB). Our lives will be balanced. So will our BYW organizations. As individuals and as a group, we Baptist Young Women will bring glory to our Lord.

"May the God of peace provide you with every good thing you need in order to do his will, and may he, through Jesus Christ, do in us what pleases him. And to Christ be the glory forever and ever! Amen" (Heb. 13:20-21 TEV).

REPROGRAM Repeat from memory all ten previously memorized verses: Ephesians 2:10; 2 Timothy 2:21; Colossians 3:12; 1 Peter 2:9-10; 1 Timothy 4:12; Romans 12:3; 1 Samuel 15:22; Psalm 119:131; Ephesians 6:18; 2 Kings 7:9.

RESPOND Flip back through this book and reflect on the things God impressed on your heart as you read. Personalize Ephesians 2:10 ("For I am God's workmanship," etc.). Thank God for the truths of that verse. In the flyleaf of your Bible, write a prayer committing yourself, from this day forward, to be all Christ has created you to be and to do all God has planned for you to do. Reference Ephesians 2:10. Date your prayer.

About the Writer

Deborah P. Brunt is a freelance writer living in Corinth, Mississippi. She received her Bachelor of Arts degree from the University of Mississippi with majors in English and Theater, and a minor in Music. Deborah has also done graduate studies at the University of Mississippi.

She is presently the mission study chairman for the Baptist Women organization at the Tate Street Baptist Chruch, and is the former church Baptist Young Women president and the associational BYW director. She has also served as the recording secretary for the Mississippi Woman's Missionary Union Executive Board.

She has had more than 60 articles published in Christian and regional magazines including extensive writing for Woman's Missionary Union. She and her husband, Jerry, have two daughters.